# Christianity in North East India

## About the Author

**Dr Grace Laltlinzo** is teaching in the Department of Social Work, Indira Gandhi National Tribal University—Regional Campus, Manipur. She has authored two books, *Pregnancy and HIV/AIDS: Exploring Women's Experiences,* 2013, *Gender from a Christian Perspective: A quest for Partnership*, 2015 and Co-edited three books, *Hybridising Theory and Practices: Social Work Towards Meeting the Challenges of Global and Local,* 2013, *Human Security in the North East India: Challenges and Predicaments*, 2015 and *Violence against Women in North East India*, 2017. Her areas of academic research and interest include social work, gender studies, health and child development.

# Christianity in North East India

## A Cultural Response

Grace Laltlinzo

CONCEPT PUBLISHING COMPANY PVT. LTD.
NEW DELHI-110059

ISBN-13: 978-93-88937-01-6

First Published 2019

*Published and Printed by*

Concept Since 1974

**Concept Publishing Company Pvt. Ltd.**
A/15-16, Commercial Block, Mohan Garden,
New Delhi-110059 (INDIA)
*T*: 91 11 25351460, 91 11 25351794
*E*: publishing@conceptpub.com; *W*: www.conceptpub.com

**Cataloging in Publication Data**--Courtesy: D.K. Agencies (P) Ltd. <docinfo@dkagencies.com>

**Laltlinzo, Grace, author.**
Christianity in North East India : a cultural response / Grace Laltlinzo.
pages cm
Includes bibliographical references and index.
ISBN 9789388937016

1. Christianity—India, Northeastern. 2. Tribes—India, Northeastern—Religion. 3. Missions—India, Northeastern. 4. Christianity and culture—India, Northeastern. I. Title.

LCC BR1156.N67L35 2019 | DDC 275.41 23

# Preface

This book is the outcome of the study on 'A Critique of the Western missionaries approach and its subsequent effect on the Tribal Cultures of the North East India' sponsored by ICSSR.

The first chapter gives the historical narration of the coming of Christianity among North East regions of India. It is a comprehensive historical narration of the various missions of the Western Christianity who came to the NE region. This chapter serves as the backgrounds of the following unfolding chapters.

The second chapter deal with the research questions which the author tackles followed by the methodology which the author apply in this study, scope and significance of the research.

The third chapter is a review of literature on some of the important books highlighting the importance of the particular studies.

The fourth chapter gives an in-depth analysis of the Western Missionaries Approach by looking at the coming of the Western missionaries to various parts of NE India. It looks and critically examines their attitude and thought process in coming to evangelise the people of NE India. It also subject the Western mentality and their various upbringing components to a strict drill of scholarly digging, whether or not they come with the view to control and change the mentality of the people of NE, or if they come with a genuine desire to share the Gospel of Christ with them.

The fifth chapter deal with the Tribal Christian and their Mission Strategy which is basically an attempt to find out comparatively if and how far were they being influenced by the Western missionaries. It first traces the history of the various church denominations and highlights the paradigm shifts in the history of Christian mission. It outlines how mission work started within the various churches and examine exactly what were the aims and objectives of doing mission among the other people. It also analyses the mission of the larger denomination among the NE Christianity from the perspective of a post-colonial approach.

The concluding chapter formulate a Proposal for Mutual Co-existence: Cultural Response to Westernization. The purpose of this final section is to reformulate or recreate a new and relevant understanding by using various Sociological theories as well as some of the Missiological theories in order to create and come up with a new paradigm wherein the tribal Christian of the North East India would finally realize their place in the overall economy of the nations.

I would also like to express my gratitude to my research Assistant Royal Lalsangthang and Dr Samson Chiru who saw me through this book; talked things over, read, offered comments, assisted in the editing, proof reading and designed.

# Acknowledgements

I am indebted to many institutions and people for their support in the framework of this research. This research project was funded by Indian Council of Social Science Research (ICSSR), New Delhi.

My special thanks goes to my University, particularly to the Vice Chancellor Prof. T.V. Kattimani, Prof. Alok Shrotriva, Dean of Social Science and Director (Academic) and staffs at the regional Campus, Manipur for giving me the academic space to complete the research project.

I also gratefully acknowledge the precious support of Prof. Laldena, whose contribution in stimulating suggestions and encouragement helped me to corordinate my research project and my research team Dr. Samson Chiru, Royal Lalsangthang and Jamkhothang Haokip for enabling me to publish this book.

I am also grateful to the respondents of the study (individuals, organizations, staffs at theological colleges) who helped me during the field-work and also in locating literatures for the study.

Lastly, I cannot get stronger words than say "Thank You" to my husband for his love and ceaseless support right from the beginning till the end.

# Contents

# Abbreviations

| | |
|---|---|
| AAM | Arthington Aborigin Mission |
| ABMU | American Baptist Missionary Union |
| AD | Anno Domini |
| BC | Before Christ |
| BMS | Baptist Missionary Society |
| EBMS | English Baptist Missionary Society |
| GoI | Government of India |
| ICSSR | Indian Council of Social Science Research |
| ILP | Inner Line Permit |
| NSCN-IM | Nationalist Socialist Council of Nagalim (Isaac-Muiva) |
| NE | North East |
| NEI | North East India |
| NT | New Testament |
| RC | Roman Catholic |
| SDA | Seventh Day Adventists |
| WPM | Welsh Presbyterian Mission |
| ZHA | Zeliangrong Heraka Association |

# 1
# The Historical Narration of the Coming of Christianity Among North East Regions of India

## Brief Sketch about North East India

The nineteenth century was the great century for Western Christian missions. Missionaries were held in high esteem for their contribution to the enlightenment of non-Western peoples. But in the twentieth century, missions became the whipping boy of secular post-modern critics. In a drastic swing of the pendulum, the social sciences began to deny their own Enlightenment theories about civilizing the so-called primitive cultures. Absolute cultural relativism and cultural absolutism became the order of the day. Changing another culture in any way, especially the religion, was deemed cultural genocide. Missionaries came in for an exceptionally large share of the blame. Now, however, going beyond the post-modern critique, scholars who are converts of the modern missionary movement and others are calling for a more objective, fair evaluation of it.

Today the total population of Tribal in India is 85-95 million and form about 9-10 per cent of India's total population and about 25 per cent of the total Christian population in India is Tribal Christian (Downs, 2003:204). This means that the tribals are among the most responsive groups of people in India. The north-east India is located in the far eastern corner of India bordering Myanmar in the east, China and Bhutan in the north, and Bangladesh in the south. The region is comprised of seven states, which are home to large indigenous/tribal communities comprising many tribes and ethnic groups with their own languages, ways of life, and histories. As it has been rightly described, the north-east India is a nation within a nation in which more than one hundred ethnically diverse groups live.

In relation to India, the north-east states are connected with the rest of the country by a narrow strip of land that is often called chicken neck—because it is long and narrow. However, this narrow strip of land has come to symbolise much more than virtually meatless part of chicken's anatomy; the real significance of this "neck" is that it symbolises the profound isolation, neglect, and exploitation the people of this region suffer. The alienation, exploitation, and neglect resulting from decades of underdevelopment have produced far-reaching consequences in the lives of the people. The lack of substantial development projects on the one hand, and the processes of globalisation on the other, have created precarious and even deadly situations for the majority of these people.

Ethnologically, the tribals in the north-east India belong to the Tibetan-Burman speaking group. In general, the tribes can be categorised as comprising two broad divisions—the hills tribes and the plains tribes. The hills tribes consist of various groups of the Mizo-Kuki-Chin family, Nagas, Khasis, Garos, and Arunachalis and they reside in the states of Mizoram, Tripura, Nagaland, Manipur, Meghalaya, and Arunachal Pradesh respectively. Most of the hills tribals have been heavily Christianised with the exception of Arunachalis who have been isolated and protected from the influence of Christian missionaries by the Indian government. Prior to their conversion to Christianity, the tribals practiced what can be called a primal religion, which is very often incorrectly classified as animism. In contrast, the plains tribals are concentrated primarily in the Brahmaputra and Barak Valleys of Assam, Manipur Valley and plains in Tripura. Most of these tribals have been converted back to Hinduism and assimilated into the Hindu culture, but some have been more strongly influenced by Islam.

## The Arrival of Christianity to the Various Tribes of North East India

The coming of Christianity in the North East can be traced back before the advent of British rule. Catholic priests were operating in the North Eastern Region of India prior to the East India Company foundations of formal empire as early as 1626, the earliest recorded visit to the region was by two Jesuit missionaries, Fr Stephen Cacella and Fr John Gabrial (Sangma, 1987). It is to be noted that though the Catholics were the foremost among Christian missionaries in the North Eastern Region, there is no account of their involvement in the establishment of their faith, they did not start any mission work in the North East region during the seventeenth century, they were probably looking for a passage to Tibet and China. They began their mission work in the region only in the early middle part of the twentieth century. The onset of missionaries in the North Eastern region has its metaphorical link with the 'Treaty of Yangdabo'. On 24 February, 1826, Assam was subjugated by the British East India Company after the treaty of Yangdabo (Puthenpurakal, 1998:207). Ten years after Assam was under the colonial rule, on 23rd March, 1836; two American Baptists, Nathan Brown and Oliver T. Cutter, arrived with their families at Sadiya, the easternmost point of Assam (now in the Lohit district of Arunachal Pradesh), who were probably heading to the Chinese Empire believing they had been led to a fruitful place, they began to learn the local language; Assamese, they later translated and published the English version of the New Testaments into Assamese. Thus, the work of the missionary in the North Eastern corner of India sees its beginning.

The pioneer Christian missionaries in the North Eastern Region of India can broadly be categorized into two major denominations namely; The Catholics and the Protestant Churches because Catholism and Protestantism were the religions of the European Colonial powers (Melvin and Sonnenburg, 2003). The Christian mission work in North East India got intensified gradually under several protestant missions and the Catholic Mission.

The American Baptist Missionary Union (ABMU) occupied Assam in 1836 simply as a step towards entering China from the West. The English Baptist Missionary Society (EBMS) were the first to do any work in Assam. Dr. Carey translated the New Testament into Assamese, and the missionaries in 1797 made one mission tour, at least, to Bhutan, and to places in Assam. Mr. Lish of the Serampore Mission laboured among the Khasis for a few years shortly previous to 1841, the date of the beginning of the present Welsh Mission. In 1876, work was begun by this society in Cachar, and was continued for some years. In 1881, Rev. I. Allen was labouring there with two native assistants. The Christian community numbered 285, with 25 communicants, and 16 adult baptisms in that year. The Assam and Cachar Mission began work in 1868, but was afterwards discontinued.

The Church of England has been conducting mission work, to some extent, in Dibrugarh and Gauhati. As non-ordained or lay agents are mentioned in the statistical tables prepared by the Calcutta Missionary Conference in 1881, it can be inferred that this work was all done through the Chaplain of Assam. In 1871, 150 were reported as belonging to the Native Christian community at Dibrugarh, but no communicants are reported. No report is given for 1881. At Gauhati the Christian community numbered ten in 1871, and eight in1881, with three communicants. The Indian Home Mission Society can hardly be said to be labouring at all among the people of Assam. They have here only a colony, and so a kind of branch of their most interesting and prosperous work among the Santals (Mathur, 1979).

The first tribe that received Christianity was the Khasis. The first contacts with them were made by the Serampore Mission at Syhlet (now in Bangladesh) in 1813, Guwahati in 1829, and at Cherapunji in 1832. No substantial results have been found although few Khasis were baptized. A more substantial and lasting interaction took place beginning in 1841 with the coming of the missionaries of the Welsh Presbyterian Mission (WPM), the first church among the tribals of India was planted in Nongsawlia, Meghalaya in 1846. In 1866, 65 schools with 2,000 pupil were established in every Shiemship except one. Teacher Training School was established at Nongsawlia in 1867. The Khasi Christians were organized into Presbytery in 1887 and in the same year the Cherra Theological College was established. A dispensary was established by Dr. Griffith in Mawphlang in 1878. The turn of the century saw the Khasi Christians growing steadily. The 1905 revival among them accelerated the numerical growth tremendously (Puthenpurakal, 1998:213). An independent and ecclesiastical Church of God was established in 1902 by Revs. Wolley M. Roy, J.J.M. Nichols-Roy, Mr. Jobin Roy Khain, Mr. Dhorum and others. It has become the third largest denominational church among the Khasis (Snaitang, 1998:239). There are substantial Seventh Day Adventists (SDA) and other smaller indigenous groups of Protestant Christians among the Khasis.

The Roman Catholics have introduced Christianity in some parts of North East India early. But only in 1889 more substantial work in the North East India was done by the Roman Catholic (RC) when the Prefecture Apostolic of Assam, Bhutan and Manipur was created. The Roman Catholics entered the Khasi hills in 1892. The two World Wars have disrupted the Catholic works more than any others. However, after the Second World War, the Catholic missions picked up where it left off, and made many outstanding contributions in the areas of education and medical works. It has gained numerous adherents among the Khasis (Puthenpurakal, 1998:213).

Significant missions began among the Garos of Meghalaya through two Garos, Omed Watre Momin and Ramkhe Watre, who were baptized on 8 February, 1863 at Guwahati. Two returned to the Garo hills to evangelise their own people in 1864. Following them the American Baptist Mission established its station in Tura in 1877. The Garo Baptist Association was established in 1875. By the turn of the century, there were about 10,000 members in the Garo Christian community. The Roman Catholic Missions (1931), the Church of England (1935) and the Seventh Day Adventists (1950) also entered into the fray. According to K.C. Marak, these three missions worked among the Garo Baptists and not among the non-Christian Garos (Snaitang, 2000).

The first encounter between Western missionaries and the Nagas took place in January 1839, when an American Baptist missionary named Miles Bronson went to the Namsang Nagas in what is now Arunachal Pradesh. However, this mission did not succeed and was terminated two years later. In March 1872, E.W. Clark established a mission station among the Aos at Molung. Subsequently, missions were started among other Naga tribes. The American missionizing enterprise was significantly truncated with India's independence in

1947. Under the mandate known as the Assam Disturbed Areas Act, 1955, the Indian Government summarily expelled all foreigners including the last American missionary. Missionary work began in Nagaland by the American Baptists in the 1870s among the Aos (Longchar, 1998:248). The earliest missionaries were Godhula Brown, an Assamese evangelist employed by the American Baptists, and the American Baptist missionary E.W. Clark. The first baptism in Naga soil took place on 23 December, 1872. Due to the diversity of the Naga tribal groups in terms of languages and culture, progress of Christianity was slow in Nagaland in the first few decades. Except for members of the Ao tribe, large numbers of the Nagas did not turn to Christianity until the third and fourth decades of the twentieth century. An interesting element in the Christianization of Nagaland is that several Naga tribes such as the Konyak, the Sangtam, and the Chang were not administered by the British, and the Government did not allow missionary work among them. However, beginning in the 1930s, the evangelization among these un-administered tribes began and after the Indian Independence, they experienced fast growth. Now the Nagas claim a hundred per cent Christianity, both in and around Nagaland (Longchar, 1998:251).

During the last decade of the 19th century missionary work began in Mizoram, first by J.H. Lorrain and F.W. Savidge of the Arthington Aborigin Mission (AAM) in 1894 were replaced by D.E. Jones of the Welsh Presbyterians in 1897. Christianity was first preached among the Mizos in 1891 by a Welsh missionary named William Williams, against the background of primitive animism, shrouded by superstitions and fears. Williams could not stay for long in the Mizo Hills, but his appeal to the Presbyterian Church of Wales resulted in the adoption of Mizo Hills as one of its mission fields. However, before the church in Wales could send a missionary, unaware of the fact that it had been adopted by the Presbyterian Church of Wales, two Arthington missionaries, J.H. Lorrain and F.W. Savidge arrived in Mizoram in 11th January, 1894 and remained for almost four years. The first Welsh missionary, D.E. Jones, arrived on 31st August, 1897 and stayed with the Arthington missionaries until their departure of that year. Edwin Rowlands joined D.E. Jones in 1898 and the two missionaries devoted most of their time to preaching tours all over Mizoram with its difficult terrain, its wild animals and forests. The missionaries worked with unsparing fervour and as soon as they won over a handful of Mizo converts they left much of the preaching ministry to the Mizos, and they gradually devoted themselves towards administration (Rees, 2002).

In Manipur, mission was started in 1894 by William Pettigrew of the Arthington Aborigin Mission, who later joined the American Baptists. In 1903, the English Baptists (Baptist Missionary Society founded by William Carey) began work in the southern part of Mizoram, when the former pioneer missionaries Lorrain and Savidge made their station in Serkawn, near Lunglei. In 1907, R.A. Lorrain, the brother of J.H Lorrain, established an independent mission agency—called the Lakher Pioneer Mission and began work among the Maras of them southern part of Mizoram. Other denominational churches entered Mizoram—Salvation Army (1921), The Roman Catholics (1925), the Seventh Day Adventists (1941) and later the United Pentecostal Church (1949). The dominion denominations among the Mizo are the Presbyterian and the Baptist Christian (Hrangkhuma, 1998:271-2).

In 1991, the three hills tribal states were dominantly Christian as follows—Meghalaya—64.8 per cent for the whole state; (Garo—66.86% and Khasi—60%, Mizoram 85.73% and Nagaland 87.47%. The non-Christians in Mizoram and Nagaland are mostly non-Mizo and non-Naga respectively. The percentage of Christians in Manipur in 1991 was 34.11. Most of the tribals in Manipur are Christians. According to K.C. Marak, the Garo Christians now are 82.50 per cent of the Garo population in Meghalaya (Snaitang, 2000). According to Joseph Puthenpurakal, during the decade ending in 1995, the Presbyterian and the Roman Catholic added new Khasi converts averaging 6,000 and 12,000 respectively every year (Puthenpurakal, 1998:206). Besides this, there are a number of indigenous Christian groups in North East India (Snaitang, 2000).

The Bodos of Assam received the Gospel in the middle of the 19th century. Apinta embraced Christianity in 1849 at Guwahati while studying in the Baptist Boarding School founded by Mr Barker, to become the first Bodo Christian. The Anglicans took over a small mission station at Tezpore in 1847/8. When Rev. Sydney Endle arrived in Assam in 1864, there had already been some Bodo converts at Tezpore (Allen, 2002:3).

The Lutheran Mission began its work in Western Assam bordering West Bengal, based in a colony in Mornai where some Santhal migrants worked in a Tea Estate during the 1870s. L.O. Skefsrud and Hans Boerresen began to concentrate their work in the neighbouring areas and in the process one Teklo Bodo became Christian on the 7th of January, 1887. The outcome of this mission was the Northern Evangelical Lutheran Church with a membership of 25,000 with 180 congregations and 1,00,000 total Christian population in 2005. In 1927, the American Baptist Missionaries established mission station at Tukhrajar, which was taken over by the Australian Baptist Missionary Society and Goalpara Bodo Baptist Christian Association has grown into a church with a membership of 10,000 baptized members (22,000 Christian community) in 155 congregations in 2005 (Basumatari 2005: 46). In the 1960s, the Roman Catholic Church also began to work among the Bodos from a Mission station at Bengtol now in Chirang district.

The Bodo Baptist Convention, originally formed as the Mongoldoi Baptist Christian Association in 1914, have 25,086 baptized membership in 268 congregations in 2005 (Pranay Daimary 2005:58). Most of the Protestant Bodo churches joined in the Bodo Baptist Board in 1955. The aim of the BCB is "Translation and revision of the Bodo Bible. Development of the Bodo Literatures, particularly Christian Literatures." (Clow, 1945: 62).

The Karbi of Assam received the gospel in 1859 through the American Baptist missionaries. The growth of Christianity among them was extremely slow during the 19th century. The first church was organised in the eastern Karbi Anglong at Chekso in 1905. At present there are 8 associations under the Karbi Anglong Baptist Association. The KABA is under the constituent of the Council of Baptist Churches in North East India (CBCNEI). The Roman Catholics (1914) and the Presbyterians (1880) also worked among the Karbis.

The tribes in Tripura received the gospel mostly in the 20th century. The Mizos in Tripura were first evangelised by Mizo Christians from Mizoram. They in turn evangelised their related tribes of Darlong and other Halam groups of people. The New Zealand Baptists began work in Tripura mostly among the Garos and the Mizo groups in 1938. The Zoram Baptist Mission began work among the Tripuri groups such as Jamatia, Noatian, Debbarma and the Riang since 1970. Now several churches are working in Tripura, some in co-operation with the Tripura Baptist Christian Union, the major denominational Church in Tripura.

Christianity began among the Rabhas of Assam in 1939 when Konoran Rabha was baptised. As a result of his witness, 25 Rabhas became Christians. However, since they could not find any church to join, 23 of them reverted back to their Rabha religion.

Thousands of missionaries, both Roman Catholics and Protestants, touched the culture of the North East of Indian tribes. Along with the new Western knowledge that greatly benefited the mass of India, came the fierce attacks of the early Christian missionaries on Hinduism and Hindu society. Given the chance, they never failed to point their fingers or scorn at ancient Hindu religion and social institutions. As a result many young Indians drifted towards Christianity. But as B.N. Luniya correctly observed, "in the long run vigorous activities of the missionaries and their vehement critic of Hindu religion and society served to rouse Hinduisms from its slumber." (Robinson & Clarke, 2003:362). And sadly after so many years the repercussion could be felt still in contemporary India.

It is clear that the tribals have been much more open to the gospel and Christianization has been, we might say, completed in such tribes as the Mizos and the Nagas where it is claimed that the entire tribes have become Christian. In such tribes, serious attempt begin to appear to contextualize Christian theology and inculturation of the church has been vigorously going on. In the older tribal churches such as among the Oraon, the Mundas and the Kharias in central India, and the Garos and Khasis in Meghalaya, where the entire members of such tribes have not embraced Christianity, the same progress in terms of contextualization of theology and inculturation of the church have been taking place. It seems to be a matter of a short time when the entire Garo tribe will become Christian. It may take more time for the Khasis to complete Christianization with the resurgence of traditional Khasi religion. The Bodo Christians are active in working together to make unique contribution in the progress of their country, and the preservation of some of their valuable cultural elements. The Christians are concerned to preserve their beautiful culture and are working to Christianize their culture (Mathur, 1979). It is hopeful that other tribes where Christianity has made inroad will continue to grow.

## References

Allen, B.C. (2001). *Gazetteer of Bengal and North East India*, reprinted New Delhi: Mittal Publications.

Andrew, G. Clow (1945). *The Future of the Assam Tribal People*, Shillong.

Downs, S. Fredericks, (2003). *History of Christianity in India,* Vol. V, Part 5, Bangalore.

Hrangkhuma, F. (eds.) (1998). *Christianity in India: Search for Liberation and Identity*, Delhi: CMS/ISPCK.

Jones, E.D. (1915). *A Lushai Primer: The Welsh Presbyterian Mission*, Aizawl.

Joshi, V.A. (2012). *Matter of Belief: Christian in Conversion Healing in North East India*, New York & Oxford: Berghmann Books.

Lonchar, Wati (1998). *The Tribal World View Ecology*, Jorthart Assam, Eastern Theological College.

Mathur, P.R.G. (1979). *The Khasi of Meghalaya: Study in Tribalism and Religion*, New Delhi.

Phukan, Basumatary (2005). *An Introduction to the Boro Language*, New Delhi: Mittal Publications.

Ponger, Imchen (1993). *Ancient Ao Naga Religion*, New Delhi.

Puthenpurakal, J. (eds.) (1996). *Impact of Christianity on North East India,* Shillong: Vendrame Institute Publication.

Rees, D. Ben (ed.) (2002). *Vehicles of Grace and Hope: Welsh Missionaries in India —1800-1970*, William Carey Library.

Robinson, Rowena and Sathianathan Clarke (eds.) (2003). *Religious Conversion in India: Modes, Motivations, and Meanings,* New Delhi: Oxford University Press.

Snaitang, O.L. (1990). *A Study of the Role of Christianity in Social Change*

*Among the Khasi and Jainitia Hills of Meghalaya from 1841 to the Present*, United Theological College, D.Th. Dissertation.

Snaitang, O.L. (eds.) (2000). *Churches of Indigenous Origins in North East India*, Delhi: ISPCK.

Syiemlieh, David R. (ed.) (2014). *On the Edge of Empire: Four British Plans for North East India —1941-1947*, New Delhi: Sage India.

# 2
# Research Rationale and Methodology

The History of Christianity in North East India is about 150 years. Different mission societies from the West came and started their works from the 19th century onwards. The Welsh Calvinistic Methodist Foreign Mission (later renamed as the Welsh Presbyterian Mission) began their works as early as the 1841 among the Khasi and among the Mizo in 1891. The American Baptist Mission started their work among the Garos in 1863 and in 1872 among the Nagas. In the southern part of Mizoram, the British Baptist Missionary Society also started their work and all these were later on added by the presence of Roman Catholics.

The attitude of the Western missionaries, Christian missions no matter from which denomination or societies they come from, all considered themselves superior and consistently maintained an exclusive attitude towards the traditional religion and cultures. They came with a strong view to conquer other world by Christian faith. One striking example can be seen from the school text-book prepared by one of the leading pioneer missionary D.E. Jones who was regarded as the friendliest among the missionaries by the Mizos. In his book, *A Lushai Primer*, is written, "There are five great races—the blacks, the reds, the browns, the yellow and the whites. But we all are one race; the yellow are most populous and the white are wisest and most superior" (Jones, 1915:32). According to their mindset, conversion was seen in terms of replacement of the old ways of life and replacing them with their own system. For them, the tribals were marauders, head hunters, barbarians and savages and they must do away with their cultures and embrace the Western missionaries' cultures as it is the standard culture. That culture is a vehicle and not the end of the communication of the Gospel seems to elude their thinking.

Therefore, a comprehensive condemnation and prohibition of activities associated with the old religion led to the destruction of many traditional cultural and customary practices of the people of North East India. This seemingly lack of regards and thinking that one's own culture is superior seems to be the norm even among the indigenous tribal Christian missions at present. Everywhere one looks the strategy adopted by different missions seems to be a mirror image of what the Western missionaries had done to them in the first place. This creates a sense of 'spiritual colonization' and in many areas one can see the adverse effect and people coming out to defend their God given cultures and traditions.

It is possible that during the colonial period missionaries with their zeal and sense of sacrifice compounded by their lack of cultural and anthropological understanding of their converts and of Biblical interpretation could have created this problem. Failing to comprehend that the Bible was written in a given social context that need to be reinterpreted to suit the present context, they had probably assumed that the 'heathen' people had to give up most if not all of their old culture together with their ethos, values and practices to follow Christ. If this trend continues and is allowed to do so, then one can see that there would be more trouble times ahead as is evident from so many conversion related problems.

## Conceptualizing the Term 'Western Missionaries Approach' and 'Tribals of the North East India (NEI)'

Christianity is of an Asian Middle East origin, but somehow it became synonymous with the Western world. When one talks of the Western world, one usually means the land belonging to the North American continent and Europe. Even though Christianity had come to India as early as the 50s Common Era, it hardly causes a stir. But when the Western missionaries came, one cannot help but notices. In the process of Christianizing the natives, they used a 'supra' and 'super-cultural' approach by which they think their culture superior over the other and believe that their culture is what a Christian culture should be.

The tribals of North East India (NEI), numbering more than 200 tribal groups belonged mainly to the Mongolian race and speak the languages/dialects of the Tibetan-Burma group. In the initial stage, they do not call themselves tribal, rather they were identified by the names of their respective communities like Naga, Mizo, Khasi, Garo, etc. They have some common characteristics namely; common ownership and sharing of goods, egalitarian lifestyle, minimum interaction with the others, and adherence to and pride in their tribal traditions and cultures.

### Objectives of the Study

The major objectives of the proposed study are:

1. To critically analyze the approach used by the Western missionaries in their attempt to Christianize the people of the North East India;
2. To examine the different missions strategy of the tribal Christian missions in North East India;
3. To be able to find out the root cause of the conversion related problem among the different tribes of North East India;
4. To find out why there are so much hesitation especially among the youth of North East India in terms of traditional acceptance and continuance;
5. To be able to shed a light on the identity crisis being faced by the people of North East India;
6. To discuss the possibility that the major problems faced by North East tribals are somehow co-related with and influenced by the Western missionaries approach;
7. To be able to show that a different approach other than the one used by the Western missionaries is not only possible but far rewarding.

### Hypothesis

Tribal society had undergone a drastic change over a period of time and is continuing to merge onward. Today, the tribal society is moving between two set poles—adoption and rejection. Traditional cultural values are adopted while some are rejected, all the while the deciding factor of what gets to be adopted and what gets to be forgotten seems to be the standard laid down by the Western missionaries. It is the researcher/researcher's hypothesis that all the problem being faced by the people of North East India—be it the depreciation of their cultures, the easily adoption of the Western cultures, the identity crisis, being rootless, the cultural imposition through Christian missions of other North East tribals and the supposedly conversion related problem, burning of church buildings, losing lives and ex-communication of one's own family members—all these stems from the misconception of believing that whatever the Western missionaries approach was used was thought to be the best and therefore worthy of emulating, but all the while seriously flawed and the consequences which we are still reeling from.

## Research Design and Methodology

Given the above hypothesis, the proposed study focus on the Western missionaries, the historical background that led to the North East India being exposed to the rest of the world and the subsequent arrival and the manner of approach being used by them in their attempts to convert the natives of the North East India. It then further analyzes the present natives Christian missions and their strategy being used. It analyzes in details taking into account all the information gathered from the different places of the North East India. Therefore, taking into consideration the proposed study, it is felt that a socio-historical approach as well as an anthropological approach be used as the methodology aided by the post-colonial approach which are further substantiated by the various sociological tools. And also the fact that this proposed research study is intrinsically related to a religious body, it is felt that an interdisciplinary approach will serve it better still to offer this research comprehensiveness.

## Tools Used in Collection of Data

Sources of information are obtained from the many native Christian missions scattered every nook and corner of the North East India. There are Tribal Centers in the various theological seminaries and colleges. Besides these, there are many other libraries where information can be obtained and where their archives which contain valuable letters and correspondents from the first Western missionaries to arrive in North East India could be held. An intensive field study will also be conducted by visiting the many missions scattered everywhere in the different states of the North East India. First hand interviews of eyewitness and interacting with many specialists in this field will hardly be overlooked.

## Significance of the Study

It would not be a gross exaggeration to say that the introspection of the tribal people of the North East India is gaining momentum very fast. Everywhere one turns, one can see various workshop being organized, papers presented and articles and books written and published about the importance of tradition and cultural ethos and how to safeguard them. Almost all the master thesis and doctoral thesis both from a secular and theological section can be seen the significant of our culture for our survival. The introduction of Tribal Theology as branch of Liberation Theology and the establishment of Tribal University, these are all pointers on how serious is felt by the people of NEI and the government at large in safeguarding the uniqueness of each and every cultural aspects of the different tribes of the North East India.

## Relevance of the Study to the Needs of Present Society

The identity crisis, the conversion related problems, the breaking of families, the devaluation of cultures and the overmagnification of Western cultures—all these are relevant problems being faced by our present societies. We try our best to come up with solutions but it proves unsatisfactory. It is highly probable that we lack focus not because we lack in zeal, infrastructure or in vision, but precisely because we are in the dark to know the root cause of our problems. Therefore, it is believed that this project study which attempt to find the root cause of our present malady would truly shed light in our deepest darkest hours. As one goes on becoming well after the problem is diagnosed correctly, the people of North East India will begin on the course of healing once it has been brought to light the root cause of our problem. Knowing what ails us will help us to formulate a solution and this is what this study hopes to achieve.

Christianity and Christian missions, therefore, in basic theological and historical terms, have consisted of individualized and institutionalized expressions of such belief. They embody both commitment and obligation. They are the continuous, ongoing, and still unfinished work by God within the heart and mind of each person and within the culture of every people. This work, carried out through the agency of imperfect human beings, both as individuals and as institutions, is an ongoing process. In every age and in every place on earth, persons converted or turned around by the agency of God's Spirit have been obliged to carry this message to those who have not yet received it. This obligation, as embodied in the Great Commission, is deemed to be the ultimate Christian mandate. As such, it still remains in force.

Yet, one of the most lingering, persistent, and stubborn misperceptions, both in India and in the West, is the notion that Christianity is essentially European and that European religion has traditionally been Christian. Of course, neither of these notions is true. Contradictions arising from such misconceptions are so manifold that they need hardly be elaborated upon further. As applied to India (or South Asia generally), the terms "colonial", "colonialism", and "colonialist" have now become the pejorative devices or epithets of choice. In relation to Christianity, Christian mission, or even to all things Christian, the term has been useful for categorically demonizing or epitomizing evil and exploitation, for assigning guilt, or for categorizing anything deemed to be "anti-national." Its essence is to be found in charges of forced conversion and proselytization. In the historiography of modern India, both as practiced in the East and in the West, the grip of the conceptual apparatus related to the perspective of this term remains firm.

## Conclusion

Throughout the history of Christianity in India can be traced back at least to the 4th century A.D., but very often it is considered as an offspring of Western colonialism. It cannot be denied that missionary work in India was done mainly during this colonial period. In the prevalent presence of the Western form of Christianity in India, it has led to the question of the identity of Christians in India.

Already in the nineteenth century many Christians were becoming aware of the fact that Christianity was a source for new identity for themselves and their notion was frustrated by their new religious 'foreignness'. They also felt a tension between their pride in being Indians and their acceptance of Christianity, the religion of the colonial ruler. As such this study hoped to amalgamate the various factors to churned out the best possible scenario for the present tribal Christians so as to make them feel at home in their own land.

# 3
# Literature Survey

The study of the history of the impact of Christianity and the introductions of it in the North East of India, is not a new project as some scholars have applied themselves to it and have done valuable work. In the following let us review some of the important books highlighting the importance of the particular studies.

**J.M. Lloyd, On Every High Hill. Liverpool: Foreign Mission Office, 1957.**

J.M. Lloyd, the long serving missionary in Mizoram in his book, *On Every High Hill*, (1957) makes an effort to relate Christianity to traditional culture. However, he reflects the mission's paternalistic view of certain cultural values as anti-Christian. Hence while acknowledging the conversion and deeper spiritual life of many Mizos as being the result of the revival movement, he sees the rise of "Puma zai" (traditional song), which in a modified form ultimately made its way into the revival, as a sudden resurgence of heathenism. It is very clear that Lloyd devalued the social and cultural values of Mizo society and wrote the history of mission from European imperialistic, colonial and political perspectives. His work needs to be re-examined minutely.

**Saiaithanga, Mizo Kohhran Chanchin [History of the Mizo Church]. Aizawl: Regional Theological Literature Committee, 1969.**

The most substantial book on the history of the church in Mizoram is the work of Saiaithanga, a Mizo pastor and prominent church leader, *Mizo Kohhran Chanchin* first published in 1969. This book is still the most widely read mainly because of his systematic arrangement, distinct and precise expression and comprehensive coverage of different traditions. As one of the early pastors, he had an opportunity to work closely with the Western missionaries as a theological teacher and a pastor. He was a representative of the church authorities who reflected the mission's ecclesiology in their approach to the revival movement in Mizo church. Saiaithanga did not recognize some elements of the revival particularly the traditional songs and drums, which are important factors for the development of Mizo Christianity. Instead, he characterized the revival movement as the cause of division, anarchy and the economic impoverishment of the church. Consequently, a clear dichotomy of the revival movement and the church can be identified in his work. His perspective is identical to that of J.M. Lloyd, who undoubtedly had considerable personal influence upon him.

**C.L. Hminga. The Life and Witness of the Churches in Mizoram. Serkawn: Mizoram, Literature Committee, Baptist Church of Mizoram, 1987.**

C.L. Hminga's book provides some relevant theological issues such as the transformation of the Mizo concept of God, faith and the establishment of the church and its growth and witness from the church growth perspective.

**F. Hrangkhuma, ed., Christianity in India: Search for Liberation and Identity. Delhi: ISPCK, 1998; F. Hrangkhuma and Joy Thomas, eds. Christ Among The Tribals. Kothanur, Bangalore: Fellowship of Indian Missiologists (FOIM), SAIACS Press; F. Hrangkhuma Mizoram Transformational Change: A study of the Procedures and Natures of the Mizo Cultural Change and Factors that contributed to the Change. Pasadena: Unpublished PhD Dissertation, Fuller Theological Seminary, 1989. etc.**

F. Hrangkhuma, one of the most renowned Tribal historians and theologian is a versatile contributor on terms of the relationships between Christianity and the Tribal religion as well as culture and what impacts it have. In most of his books he vividly describes the changes and transformation that have taken place in Mizoram and the rest of the North East since the coming of Christianity in Mizoram. Relevant theological issues such as concepts of God, Christ, salvation and ecclesiology can be found in this research.

**Lalrinawmi Ralte. Crab Theology: A Critique of Patriarchy, Cultural Degradation and Empowerment of the Mizo Women. Cambridge, MASS: Unpublished D. Min Thesis, 1993.**

Lalrinawmi Ralte's *Crab Theology* clearly presents a view of Mizo women as it developed out of Mizo traditional and culture. Religio-cultural issues particularly the feminist view of God are seen as relevant and valid in constructing Mizo contextual theology. It also speaks for all the tribal women's experience in North East India as the cultural and societal structure are quite homogeneous in the superficial level.

**Mangkhosat Kipgen. Christianity and Mizo Culture. Aizawl: Mizo Theological Conference, 1995.**

Mangkhosat Kipgen, a church historian published his research under the title *Christianity and Mizo Culture* which gives a historical perspective of the Mizo traditional culture and Mizo Christianity.

**K. Thanzauva, ed. Towards a Tribal Theology: The Mizo Perspective. Jorhat: Mizo Theological Conference, 1989; K. Thanzauva, Theology of Community: Tribal Theology in the Making. Aizawl: Mizo Theological Conference, 1997; K. Thanzauva. Reports of the Foreign Mission of the Presbyterian Church of Wales on Mizoram 1894-1957. Aizawl: Synod Literature and Publication Board, 1997; K. Thanzauva. Transforming Theology: A Theological Basis for Social Transformation. Bangalore: Asian Trading Corporation, 2002.**

K. Thanzauva one of the pioneer in tribal theology as contributed a lot in this field and his books will be of great help in our ongoing research. Research published under the title *Theology of Community* (1997) contributes a theological reflection on the traditions, experiences and concepts of the tribal Christians in North East India. The most significant elements of his research are the Godhead, ecclesiology and humanity.

**Lalsangkima Pachuau. Ethnic Identity and Christianity: A Socio-Historical and Missiological Study of Christianity in North East India with Special Reference to Mizoram. Frankfurt: Peter Lang Gmb H, 2002; Lalsangkima Pachuau, ed. Ecumenical Missiology: Contemporary Trends, Issues and Themes. Bangalore: UTC, 2002.**

Lalsangkima Pachuau's research entitled, *Ethnic Identity and Mizo Christianity* concentrates on ethnic identity and Christianity in North East India. It deals with the interaction between the Mizo church and traditional culture and the role of the revival movement.

**Vanlalchhuanawma, A Historical Study of the Synod Mission Board 1953-1981. Bangalore: UTC, Unpublished MTh Thesis, 1984; Vanlalchhuanawma, Revival Movement and the Church in Mizoram 1906-1949. Bangalore: UTC, Unpublished DTh Thesis, 1998; Vanlalchhuanawma, Christianity and Subaltern Culture: Revival Movement as a Cultural Response to Westernization in Mizoram. Delhi: ISPCK, 2006.**

Vanlalchhuanawma's research published clearly describes the Mizo traditional religion and cultural practices before Christianity and changes in the Mizo society. These are relevant to the present research because it deals with contextualization.

**Takatemjen. Studies on Theology and Naga Culture. Mokokchung: CTC, AOLIJEN, 1997.**

He is one of the Naga theologians who is concerned with the interaction of Christianity and the Naga culture. In his book, he attempts to understand the relationship between Theology and Culture, making an effort to do theology with the resources of socio-cultural traditions of the Naga tribes. The underlying conviction of these studies is that, in the traditional Naga culture there are values and sources for renewal of their lives and society. Drinking from the "well" of our own culture could be an answer for the problems of our day which have come to stay along with the process of modernisation. He believes that the poems, folktales, stories, dance and songs of the Naga land could be the cement of their community and they can meaningfully dialogue with the theological currents making them to come alive with a new spirituality glowing through them and not necessarily opposing each other.

**Frances F. Hiebert. Beyond a Post-Modern Critique of Modern Missions: The Nineteenth Century Revisited. Missiology: An International Review, Vol. XXV, No. 3, July 1997.**

Frances tried to find out the reason why Missionaries and the missionary movement went from respect to reproach, and now reproach is giving way to reinterpretation. What are some of the reasons for these changing perceptions? This recent contemporary trend in missiology is revising the way the modern missionary movement has been perceived by its post-modern critics.

**R.E. Welsh. The Challenge to Christian Missions: Missionary Questions and the Modern Mind. 2nd ed. London: H.R. Allenson Limited Racquet Court Fleet Street, 1906.**

This book, published way back in 1906 gives a startling insight to the problems that the missionaries have caused and encountered in their zeal to spread the good news. The writer believes that Christianity has lots of good things to offer, yet something has to be done to interpret the missionary cause. The task as here outlined is of much too great a magnitude to be fully overtaken in a little volume of ten brief chapters. It will be enough for the writer's purpose if, without going into confusing detail, he can ventilate the subject, and contribute even a little towards the provisional solution of current missionary problems. This is a good primary source to study.

**The Assam Mission: The American Baptist Missionary Union, Papers and Discussions, Jubilee Conference held in Nowgong, December 18-29, 1886. Calcutta: Published by the Assam Mission of the American Baptist Missionary Unison, 1887.**

This is a good primary source for the spread of Christianity in North east India. There are lots of interesting details on how the missionaries looked at North East and what their concerns were. It gives us the twilight insights into the Western missionaries mind set as they come to terms with the people of the North East India. This book records the minute detail of the discussion of the first missionaries to the North East it was the time where Assam covered the whole North East. The workers of the Assam Mission have always been so far separated that, though the desirability of a general conference has often been felt, no gathering of the whole Mission has taken place since 1854. It was felt that, all the workers ought to meet, review the past, compare notes on the present, and lay plans for the future. This is the outcome of the discussion being published. Some of the missionaries present were (like the who is who of today) from the American Baptist Missionary Union: Rev. C.E. Burdette and Wife from Guwahati, Rev. E.W. Clark and Wife from Molung, Rev. A.K. Gurney and Wife from Sibsagar, Rev. M.C. Mason from Tura, Rev. P.H. Moore and Wife from Nowgong, Rev. E.G. Phillips and Wife from Tura, Rev. S.W. Rivenburg and Wife from Molung, Rev. W.E. Witter and Wife from Wokha, Miss Ella C. Bond from Tura, Miss. Orrell Keeler from Nowgong, Miss. Stella H. Mason from Tura and Miss. Nettie Purssell from Nowgong. Other Societies representatives were, Rev. T. Jerman Jones, Welsh Calvinistic Methodist Mission, Shillong, Assam and Rev. Isaac F. Row, Anglo-Indian Evangelization Society, Bangalore, Deccan. Missionaries Absent, Mrs. M.R. Bronson, in U.S. Rev. C.D. King and Wife, of Kohima, en route to U.S.

**Robert Eric Frykenberg eds. Christians and Missionaries in India: Cross-Cultural Communication since 1500. Grand Rapids: Eerdmans, 2003.**

This book has several goals. It convincingly challenges the "pervasive assumption that Christianity in India is nothing more than a Western, European, or 'colonial' imposition." It documents the dynamic relationship and communication that existed between the Western church and Indian Christians. That there was active communication between Indian Christians and the European and American missionaries, that Indian Christians were able in many respects to assert their views and interpretation of the situations and problems that they confronted in their country, and that often the result was a synthesis that suited the genius of Indian culture and social and political trends are amply demonstrated in the sixteen chapters of this eminently readable and insightful book.

**Daniel Johnson Fleming. Devolution in Mission Administration: As Exemplified by the Legislative History of Five American Missionary Societies in India. New York/Chicago/Toronto/London/ Edinburgh: Fleming H. Revell Company, 1916.**

In this primary source, one finds Fleming dealing with the need for 'devolution' which is a term used to indicate the act of devolving, transferring or handing over. In the literature of missions, it is increasingly used to denote the transfer of powers, authority and responsibilities from foreign Churches and Missions to indigenous organizations. He believes that, there is no rule-of-thumb generalization that is possible giving caution that mere copying of methods used elsewhere is as unwise in the realm of racial education as in that of individual education. The first study of the teacher is the pupil. The individual men or group—their needs and nurture at the time—must be centric. There must be the recognition in actual practice that truest growth is from within and not from the absorption of ready-made ideas; that groups like individuals are to be creative and that it is activity and shouldering of responsibility that develops. This is a good source to find out the mentality of the missionaries and their mission administration in the early days.

**Joseph Paul Charles. Global Christianity: Trends in Mission and the Relationship with Non-Western Missionaries Working Cross-Culturally in Thailand. South Africa: South African Theological Seminary. Unpublished MTh Thesis, 2009.**

Even though this thesis is focussed on what happens at Thailand, nonetheless, we can use the material inside to comparatively look at some similarities that the Western missionaries faced and as well as using it for the analysis of what the future holds for missions.

**Thomas H. Lewin. A Fly on the Wheel or How I help to Govern India. London: Constable & Company LTD, 10 Orange Street Leicester Square WC, 1912.**

This is an extraordinary monograph on an encounter between the Mizo chief and the British political officers. This is a first-hand information on how the tribal of the North East Region were perceived by her majesty officers and how it can be used to compare the attitude of the first Western missionaries that come to this place. The following excerpt conveys the attitude of the tribal warriors, "Day after day passed by as we pursued our course, marching farther and farther into the bowels of the land, until by the end of the month we had reached the great Towrang Tlang range, where the General hoped to obtain some tidings of the other column. The enemy always pursued the same unsatisfactory tactics; they fought as little as possible, but burned their villages on our approach, retiring with all they could carry. They hailed us out of the jungle one day, saying, "Do not destroy our grain." "Let your chiefs come in, then", I re-joined, "and make submission." "No, no, no," was the reply. "Go your ways; leave our country. We have nothing for you but powder and ball, and plenty of that" (Thomas, 1912:272). Brave words indeed, not some people who could be looked down upon simply!

**Lawmsanga. A Critical Study on Christian Mission with Special Reference to Presbyterian Church of Mizoram. Birmingham: University of Birmingham. Unpublished PhD Thesis, 2010.**

This unpublished doctoral thesis is very relevant as it does an in-depth research in the relationship between Christianity and Mizo culture. It is in the hope that the Mizo Christianity will take deep roots in the psyche of the people that this research is done. The study explores how, as a result of the Colonial rule and the Mission enterprise, the life of the Mizo society was changed in both constructive and destructive ways. In one way it liberated the Mizos from unjust social and cultural structures in various ways. On the other hand, they started to develop the idea that all that is associated with Mizo traditional religion and culture as pagan, profane and secular and not fit for newly Mizo Christians. The author also invites the Mizo Christians to critically analyse their past religious and cultural traditions with the purpose of rediscovering and discerning the revelation of God.

**Jesse C. Fletcher. "Foreign Mission Board Strategy" in "Southern Baptist Convention Daily Bulletin", June 11, 1974.**

This is an insightful article being written. Jesse gives a lot of thought into this article and the finding as well as the analysis of the needful strategists are precious for this paper. Strategy is defined as generalship—the art of directing the larger military movements and operations of a campaign. In terms now operable at the Foreign Mission Board, it is the managing of resources for their greatest effectiveness—the relating of one part of the work to the objectives of the whole. As he look thought the various years of the southern mission foreign strategy, he wrote, "The components of strategy are many. One of the problems of isolating strategic statements through the years is a tendency on the part of some to confine strategy to mission principles or methods or objectives or philosophy. For the purpose of this paper mission strategy components include objectives, fields of labour, and types of work, management approach, personnel policies, support procedures, and goals. Actions related to any of these seven items are understood as strategic, and the aggregate of such statements constitutes strategy at any given time whether consciously recognized as such or not" (Jesse, 1974:210).

**Jesudas M. Athyal. "Gospel and Cultures: A Subaltern Reading of the History of Christian Mission in India," in http://jmathyal.tripod.com/index.html.**

This online resource reviews the modern missionary movement which became dominant in India in the eighteenth and nineteenth centuries is an important component of the current ecumenical discussions on gospel and culture. It asked searching questions such as, "What was its impact?" "Did it play a constructive or a negative role in Christian witness in India and in 'nation building'?" "What are their lessons for today?" These are among the several questions being raised.

**Lucas V. Woodford. Great Commission, Great Confusion, or Great Confession? The Mission of the Holy Christian Church. Eugene: Wipf and Stock, 2012.**

This book addresses the dichotomy that categorizes Lutherans as either "missional" or "confessional" and the underlying assumption that the two are mutually exclusive. A brief section on "Postmodern Confusion" looks at the challenges as well as the possibilities for confession present in what is commonly referred to as "Postmodernity." Assessing representatives of the church-growth movement largely from the 1990s, Woodford points out how organizational models shaped by the social sciences negatively trumped theological integrity: "Putting it bluntly a deformed Gospel can only lead to deformed Christians" (Lucas, 2012:104).

**Christoph von Fürer-Haimendorf. Tribes of India: The Struggle for Survival. Berkeley: University of California Press, 1982.**

This book tells of observations among Indian tribal populations spanning the period from 1940 to 1980. In a frank and uncompromising stand, the author posited that, "Any realistic and unbiased analysis of the present situation of the Indian tribes must inevitably contain some references to the failures as well as the successes of government policies and include also some criticism of those responsible for the misfortunes of many tribal communities. Such outspoken criticism may be considered inappropriate on the part of an observer who throughout his fieldwork has benefited from the assistance of numerous government officials. Yet no good purpose can be served by turning a blind eye to corrupt practices and the resulting failures of policies, thereby distorting the picture of the true conditions of tribal populations" (Christoph, 1982:11). This is a primary source for getting information for the various tribal cultures.

**Atul Y. Aghamkar. "Traditional Hindu Views and Attitudes Towards Christianity", Bangalore: SAIACS: Published under Featured Articles at www.globalmissiology.org, January 2008.**

This article looks at the unique relationship between the two great religions. Hindu views and attitudes toward Christianity form an extremely important but largely neglected area of study. Often, efforts have been made to find out how the Christians have approached or should approach Hindus with the gospel. Rarely is any effort undertaken to understand the Hindu point of view. Christianity never had smooth sailing in India. It often faced opposition from different segments of the Hindu community. Oppositions from the Hindus were frequently based on some partial truth, or no truth at all. Whatever their objections, the Hindus found it difficult to understand and accept Christianity as a foreign missionary religion. Numerous misconceptions about Christianity still exist in the minds of the Hindus today. One of the most often discussed and debated objections to Christianity is that it was introduced to India by Western tradesmen and missionaries.

Hindus feel that Christianity is meant for Westerners and that Hindus should not be converted to it, for Christianity is a foreign religion. Staffner brings this in to perspective when he states, "The basic understating of many Hindus is still that each country has its own religion or forms of religion. Hinduism is the religion of the people of India, Christianity is the religion of Europe and America. They regard Christianity as a religion which has been imported from outside, and is nurtured and dominated from outside" (1978:144). Therefore, on the sole ground that Christianity is a foreign and Western religion, Hindus tend to reject it.

**Rufus Anderson. History of the Mission American board of Commissioners for Foreign Mission India. Boston: Congregational Publishing, 1874.**

The American Board of Commissioners for Foreign Missions is the oldest institution in the foreign un-evangelized nations. The first mission of the Board was in India, and the history of its missions naturally commences there. Other considerations led the writer to begin with the Sandwich Islands, and then to go through with the history of the Missions to the Oriental Churches. The volumes stand properly in the following order: The India Missions, the Sandwich Islands Mission, and the Missions to the Churches. This is also a primary source.

**Robert Hunter. History of the Missions of the Free Church of Scotland in India and Africa. London/Edinburgh/New York: T. Nelson and Sons, Paternoster Row, 1873.**

This primary resource also is a stand out among the other sources in giving us the first hand information of what the missionaries and their mission board did in various parts of India. This is a detailed account of continuous history of the Free Church Missions in India and Africa. According to the author, on the reason of why he write this (we can see the prevailing mind-set of that time), About a couple of years ago, friends deeply interested in the evangelization of the heathen world, and whose judgment was deserving of the utmost respect, applied to the writer, inviting him to undertake the volume which now, with all humility, he sends forth. The primary authorities on which the greater part of the narrative is based are the Reports of the Scottish and Glasgow Missionary Societies the successive series of the Missionary Record, from its origin in May 1838 to the present time; the Scottish Christian Instructor; with various other works. Sundry facts in the early part of the volume were taken from Brown's History of the Propagation of Christianity since the Reformation; and for portions of the geographical descriptions, obligation is acknowledged to Thornton's Gazetteer of India. When unable to obtain proper details of important events, published imperfectly at the time, or not published at all, the writer sought information, and with success, from more than one of his missionary fathers or brethren.

**Julius Richter. A History of Missions in India. Translated by Sydney H. Moore. New York/Chicago/Toronto: Fleming H. Revell Company, 1908.**

Another primary source of information for the history of Missions in India that deals with the earliest time when Christianity claims its stake in the land of India. It deals with many topics in regards to the land, the people and their cultures, the problems and the success faced by Christians.

**M.A. Sherring. The History of Protestant Missions in India From their Commencement in 1706-1881. Revised an up-to-date by Rev. Edward Storrow. London: the Religious Tract Society, 56 Paternoster Row, 65 St. Paul's Churchyard, AND 164 Piccadilly, 1884.**

This important first-hand information, a primary source deals with the spread of Protestant churches in India. The aim of this work is to show historically what Protestant Missions have accomplished in India since their commencement in the beginning of the last century. This is a collected material of all the important events of these Missions which have been presented in a succinct and consecutive narrative, thus striving to give a complete view, as in a panorama, of their operations and achievements. The main focus, in short, has been to show how the wave of Christianity, commencing in one corner of the land, has gradually advanced until it has spread over the entire country.

**Nancy Ekka. Impact of Modernization on tribal Religious customs and Traditions: A Case Study of Rourkela. Rourkela: Department of Humanities and Social Sciences, National Institute of Technology Rourkela Unpublished MA Thesis, 2013.**

The objective of the study was to measure the impact of modernisation on the religious customs and traditions of the tribal residing in Rourkela. The study was confined to the four major tribes, viz. Kisan, Oraon, Kharia and Mundas, who reside in different settlements located in Rourkela. A major issue that the study reveals is the large-scale impact of modernisation and urbanisation on indigenous tribal areas of Rourkela that is rapidly eroding the age-old customs and traditions of the tribal groups. Even though the focus may not be the same, yet the topic i.e. the tribal on whom the study is based can offer interesting insight to the project as all tribal no mater where they are have a homogenous entity at least in their superficial level of existences.

**J. Puthenpurakal, eds. Impact of Christianity on North East India. Shillong: Vendrame Institute Publication, 1996.**

A wonderful collection of articles focussing on the impact of Christianity on the North East, if mainly from a Roman Catholic perspective, nonetheless crucial for this paper research. This edited work came to light because to the fact that North East India and Christianity are in the limelight these days. Politicians, academicians, socialists and religious leaders have their own perception of the region and of Christianity there. Since every impact makes a difference, it will be interesting and enlightening to listen to those who have made scholarly efforts to measure scientifically Christianity's contribution to North East India. The present volume enables the reader to have access to the findings of a cross-section of scholars addressing a wide range of issues on this theme. If being informed is important, then being informed impartially and critically is crucial. Hence, this book is valuable as it is thoroughly researched and can be utilized as a reference book and since it is a well-documented analysis of the impact that Christianity has made on North East India, it comes as one of the best resource materials to have.

**Jangkholam Haokip. "Implications of Having an Independent Missionary: A Review of the 1910 Kuki Mission", in International Bulletin of Missionary Research, vol. 38, No. 2.**

This interesting article offers quite an insight to the missionaries' activities especially among the Kuki Christians in Churachanpur, Manipur. During the latter part of the nineteenth century and the early twentieth century, Christian mission work in what is now called North East India was conducted in collaboration with the British colonial administration ten per cent. In fact, the period during which missionaries were most active in North East India, particularly in the area where the Kuki people lived, coincided with the peak of colonialism. Missionary activity in that period was based on the concept of racial and cultural superiority and was marked by the religious optimism of the West.

In this article, the contributor evaluates, from an insider's viewpoint, the work a century ago of an independent Welsh missionary, Watkin Roberts, among the Kuki, whose traditional homeland now forms parts of North East India, Burma, and the Chittagong Hill Tracts of Bangladesh. He argued that a fresh look at such independent mission enterprises can enlighten contemporary mission thinking and practice. And not only this, it also offers us a historical tit bits of these places.

**D.R. David. India Leadership study: A Summary for Indian Christian Leaders, February, 2002, in http://www.firstfruit.org.**

This online article, basing on in-depth personal interviews with approximately 300 leaders, primarily Indians, representing about 200 churches and Christian organizations, in nearly every state of India have come up with the need for further training of the missionaries as well as those Christian leaders in their efforts to reach the unreached. The indigenous missionaries, evangelists and church-planters who are establishing these congregations need to be equipped as well and trainers of trainers need to be prepared at the highest levels.

**Grace R. Lewis. The Lushai Hills: The Story of the Lushai Pioneer Mission. London: The Baptist Missionary 19, Furnival Street, 1907.**

This book, a true and rare monograph, a primary source, is an outcome of the hard work and dedication given by the author and her love for the hilly people of the Lushai Hills. This book utilizes first hand informations gleaned from the very source who had witnesses what had happened there. The author has gleaned the Lushai lore, here given, from the writings of Government experts published in Blue Books, reports of Major Shakespeare, C.I.E., D.S.O., formerly Superintendent of the Lushai Hills, letters and papers telling of their work in North Lushai hills from the Treasurer of the Assam Frontier Pioneer Mission and to the missionaries' first-hand account of their work.

**Mohan D. David. Mission, Inter-cultural encounter and change in Western India: A Case Study of Local in Relation to Global Church History, in Mission Studies, Vol. XVI-1, 31, 1999.**

This article deals with the importance of looking at the church history form the indigenous perspectives. The new phenomenon of writing global church history has arisen because mission histories until recently had been written from the western or the metropolitan point of view. But now, since most churches, especially in Asia, are no more organically connected with the Western church, from about 1950, it has become imperative to look at the history of Christianity of the non-Western world and interpret it from the indigenous point of view. This way of writing church history emphasizes the study of the local, regional or national history in its multitude of relationships, and then relates these to the experiences in similar situations elsewhere.

**Daniel Jeyaraj. "The First Lutheran Missionary Bartholomäus Ziegenbalg: His Concepts of Culture and Mission from a Postcolonial Perspective", in Swedish Missiological Themes, 93, 3 (2005).**

Jeyaraj, in this penetrating article, interacts with the notion of post-colonial reading of Christianity and her notion of mission. In postcolonial studies, the validity of meta-narratives are bitterly criticized because every narrative is local, contextual, and necessarily relative. In this context absolute claims are shunned because such claims can be imposed over against the beliefs of other people. As a result, Christian mission is considered to be an act of intrusion. The Lordship of Jesus Christ, the centrality of the Bible, the reality of conversion, the emergence of native Christian congregations, introduction of cross-cultural educational methods, intercultural encounters and the legacy of Western Christian missionaries in non-Western parts of the world are deeply suspected. Another critique of postcolonial scholars is to understand Christian mission as an act of Western colonialism. He counters the fact that this view ignores the fact that Christian mission is an integral part of Christian faith. Right from the beginning ordinary Christians, Christian monks, nuns, traders, sailors, soldiers, slaves, wandering hermits, diplomats, immigrants and others shared their understanding of Christianity with those non-Christians with whom they interacted.

**Tezenlo Thong. A Clash of Worldviews: The Impact of the Notion of Progress on Naga Culture, 1832-1947, in Journal of Race, Ethnicity, and Religion Volume 2, Issue 5 (May 2011).**

This is a massive yet scholarly article on the devalued worldviews and the rudderless and unfocused group of people namely the Naga of the North East India which resulted in their encounter with the Western Christianity. Tezenlo Thong believes that the contact between the Euro-American West and the colonized peoples, no less the Nagas, beginning with the era of European colonization and continuing today in an age of globalization, has not simply created a clash but has had grave cultural, political, physical and psychological consequences for the colonized. Consequent upon the contact with the West, the Nagas and their worldview were dismissed, stereotyped and demonized. As a result, today much of their worldview has been skewed, altered or replaced by their colonizers' worldview. Naga cultural and political structures and perspectives have been gradually eroded.

**Gunnel Cederlöf. The Politics of Caste and Conversion: Conflicts among Protestant Missions in Mid-Nineteenth Century India, in Swedish Missiological Themes, 88, 1 (2000).**

In this article, strategies adopted by different castes in a situation of increased mobility and the growing importance of mobilisation for social reforms, are points of reference for the arguments pursued.

One of the early, major conflicts between and within the different Protestant missionary societies working in south India in the earlier part of the nineteenth century was over the issues of caste and conversion. In the documents of the different missionary societies, this may appear to have been a conflict over European ideological crosscurrents, the correct creed and about making claims to converts. In other words, a controversy over the territories of power and souls in a situation where India only recently had become open to Christian missions of all kinds. However, within the Indian society in which this conflict took place, the socio-economic context was under change and this context was decisive for the course of events.

**Elungkiebe Zeliang. A History of the Manipur Baptist Convention. Imphal: Manipur Baptist Convention, 2005; Elungkiebe Zeliang. A Socio-Political and Economic History of the Zeliangrong Naga. Jorhat: Eastern Theological College. Unpublished B.D. Thesis, 2006; Elungkiebe Zeliang. "Traditional Practices and the Charismatic Movement Among the Zeliangrong Naga Baptists in North East India", in American Baptist Historical Society.**

This work is important source for the historical information to the tribe of Zeliang Naga especially in Manipur, it gives us insight into how they embrace Christianity and how they grow and interact with the outside influence as well as the interaction between their culture and how they adoped and re-defined their cultures and synthesis their previous religion to the one they embrace now, namely Christianity.

**Vumson. Zo History: With an Introduction to Zo culture, Economy, Religion and their Status as an Ethnic Minority in India, Burma, and Bangladesh. Aizawl, Mizoram, India: Published by the Author, 1986.**

This is a monumental task taken by Vumson in trying to trace the history of Zo who inhabited almost every part of the North-East regions of India. The history of the Zo people is very complex because they have many versions of legends and traditions. Their clothing, houses and diet differ from one area to another because of climatic differences within a short distance. The language, though basically similar, has developed into multi-dialects. Even their name as a people has been pronounced in many different ways. The abovesaid works are an attempt to clarify the origins of Zo people and their migration roads to their present settlements. It also seeks to trace all Zo people and pinpoint where they are to be found and the political and cultural condition they are facing today.

**Telfer Mook. Western Responsibility to a United Church in India: Recent Developments and Opportunities, in Occasional Bulletin, Vol. XII, No. 8 (October 1961).**

This article attempts to unite the different churches and mission in the West to work for a peaceful solution so that they would not be a divisive factor to the churches in India. As united churches in India, in the south and now in the north, have started and developed, the contributor calls upon the West to redefine their responsibilities. In earlier days, a comity arrangement seemed to suffice—an arrangement which set off certain geographical areas for a particular missionary board or society. But this plan is no longer suitable, either for the church in India or for the Western church. When the Western Christianity is told that the present Western mission board policy is a divisive and weakening force in the Church in India, this article seems more relevant for this particular studies.

**Herbert Hoefer. Why are Christians Persecuted in India? Roots, Reasons, Responses, in International Journal of Frontier Missions 18:1 (Spring, 2001).**

Dr. Herbert Hoefer is a former missionary to India, having served from 1968-1983 with the Lutheran Church, Missouri Synod. In his article he feels that the Christians were persecuted and their progeny also as they are the offspring of a colonial Christianity. He looks at the various factors for being persecuted.

**Donald McGavran. Wrong Strategy: The Real Crisis in Mission** is also a very important source for what happed when a mission strategy went wrong and had run its course. This article asked the ever important question: What is correct strategy in the Christian mission? This question stands at the heart of the missionary dilemma to-day. Until the major direction is determined and agreed, the effectiveness of the missionary enterprise is sorely diminished. No question is more important than this: What are the policies, patterns, goals and principles of highest urgency?

**O.L. Snaitang, eds. Churches of Indigenous Origins in North East India. Delhi: ISPCK, 2000.**

The edited work is an attempt to facilitate dialogue, openness and to foster mutual understanding and closer unity; to stimulate further knowledge and insights, to create a general awareness among people, churches and institutions and to promote peace and reconciliation. Therefore, it is anticipated that such study will be of some contribution to the larger academic research, theological education, human relationships and national integration.

**F. Hrangkhuma eds. Christianity in India: Search for Liberation and Identity. Delhi: CMS/ISPCK, 1998.**

The 15 chapters in this edited work speak of something different, on a state-wise basis. It is a study of the backward groups from various parts of India who are looking for liberation and identity, in the context of the present condition. The history of Christianity in India is a part of the socio-cultural history of the Indian people rather than as separate from it. The history will therefore focus attention upon the Christian people in India, upon who they were and how they understood themselves; upon their social, religious, cultural and political encounters; upon the changes which these encounters have produced in them and in their appropriation of the Christian gospel as well as in the Indian cultures and society of which they themselves were a part.

What are the attitudes of the Christians to their non-Christian counterparts? What is their attitude to their traditional culture and customs? Do they accept the church they belong to as their very own and are not simply participating in it? Do they accept that the survival, growth, ministry, weaknesses, etc., of their Church as their responsibility in every sense of the term, and not outsiders? Is the whole Christian community among the people group active in the ministry of the Church and not only the few salaried workers?

# 4

# The In-depth Analysis of the Western Missionaries Approach

Indian Christians trace the origin of their church of the Apostle Thomas who visited Kerala in the 1st century of Christian era. As per traditions of Kerala a colony of Syrians headed by a merchant named Canai Thomas or Thomas of Canai, came to Cranganore and settled in the city. In fact, it is said that South India, in ancient times was in contact with the Roman world. There was good deal of sea borne trade between the ports of the west coast and those on the Red Sea and the Persian Gulf. The Hebrew king Solomon (10th century B.C.) is believed to have obtained the 'ivory apes and peacocks', mentioned in the Bible's Old Testament, from the Malabar Coast. The Hebrew word for peacock is an adaptation of the Tamil 'Tukkei' (bird with splendid tail). Historians consider this as undeniable proof that the Hebrews who had no peacocks got the bird and its name from the Tamil country.

External evidences, found in the writings of the early doctors of the church, support Indian traditions. A Syriac work, believe to be of the 4th century, gives a vivid description of the work of the Apostle Thomas in the kingdom of Gundaphoros, a king who ruled in North Western India. Jerome (4th century A.D.), Gregory of Tours (6th century) and several others have references to the Apostle Thomas and his work in India. As it will be discussed in detail in the subsequent chapter, while many pleaded for the old policy of non-interference in the religious beliefs of the Indians, the government finally yielded to the pressure of the Evangelists like Wilberforce. The missionaries were permitted by the 1813 Charter Act to promote among the Indian useful knowledge and their religious and moral development.

Normally missionary's nationality was quite important so far as relationship with the government was concerned. Charles Travelyan' immediate choice was no other than the British Baptist Mission. However, unfortunately Travelyan's expectation was turned down by William H. Pearce of Baptist Missionary Society (BMS) at Calcutta when he intimated the government about his inability to undertake a new mission field as two stations were recently opened at Cheerapunji and Gauhati but suggested that the government should invite the American Baptist Mission (ABM) from Burma. As it was viewed that ABM has the prospect of opening the 'gateway to the Celestial Empire'—it would act as a highway to Tibet and western China from missionary viewpoint. It was also felt that it could serve as political and commercial purposes. Under the patronage of East India Company in the pretext of tea planting, the Gospel was taken to the extreme eastern end of the Brahmaputra valley with the twin interest of setting China Mission and the Shan Mission. The prime objective of the Mission was only a part of the Asian strategy for evangelizing the Shans and then the Chinese. The missionaries were now concerned more with evangelizing the Shans and the Chinese a sort of two birds in a bush than Assam in hand.

China Mission was a passing mission, anyway it was a mission. How it came could be traced back from the humiliation of China and subsequent signing of the treaty of Nanking after the Opium War in 1843. This opportunity was immediately seized upon by the missionaries as if it were opened by Providence for missionizing the Celecial Empire. An Englishman, David Urquhart made fun of the episode saying that 'England was offering China at the same time opium and evangelism' (Urguhrt, 2015:25). So continuous and vehement was China's hostility towards the Western missionaries that the later found no alternative than to fall back upon the western powers. In turn the dependence of missions on the government made the Chinese to think that the missionary movement was just a part of western imperialism.

Did their theology combine in any way with the ideology of colonialisms? This chapter will analyze just how far their environment is and western mentality conformed to their message of salvations? Did their theology combine in any way with the ideology of colonialisms?

## Western Colonialism and Christian Mission

Christian Mission and colonialism in nineteenth century seemed to go hand in hand in Africa and Asia. Seen in this perspective many people in Africa and Asia assumed that the role of colonialism as that of politician and a priest.

By and large, colonialism seemed to represent Christian Mission and Christian Mission appeared to be part and parcel of the Western colonialism. Which is why, Christian Missions were termed as mere hunting dog of Western imperialism. No doubt, though seemingly there lay cordial relations between Christian missions and colonialism yet, there also lay a bundle of tense discrepancies and complexities. This relationship problem depended on their mode of interactions which also differ from mission to mission and from country to country. In other words, the degree and extent of their interactions which depended on the particular mission and issues involved as well as the nature of the colonial situation. Therefore, generalization of the nature of the relation of a particular mission with a particular colonial government would be risky, and so the specific objective of this part of the study.

Missionaries can be categorized into three groups:

(i) Total collaborationists (e.g., Spain and Portugal);
(ii) Partial collaborationists (most of the tribals in Noth East India etc.); and
(iii) Non-collaborationists (China and in initially countries like Fiji, South and Central Africa, Sierra-Leone, Burma, Guinea etc.).

Certainly colonialism and Christian mission might have had what is called operational unity but in most cases the missionary was far ahead of the government and even of a backward region where a state of barbarism or savagery existed. The missionaries in Fija, South and Central Africa, Sierra Leone, Burma, Guinea, etc. emerged long before the British imperialistic had set their foothold over them. Certain tribal belts in the North East India were no exception. For instance, Rev. Pettigrew had a vision to pioneer Manipur (Major

Maxwell, the then political Agent of Manipur, lent a great help in getting Ukhrul pioneered). So were other areas in Nagaland in the second quarter of the 19th century AD (where Jenkins lent quite initial sustenance for the missionaries). But definitely before the British administrators could dare to set foot in these ethnic tribes of the North East India the missionaries did it so before. Say in the case of Rev. Pettigrew who himself was a British blood, the British officers had more confidence in him. However, in missionary movement, such as in Madagascar and Buganda, the missionaries had managed to penetrate into before and outside the realm of British colonial administration which invalidated the theory of mission without colonial protection and its indispensability. Thus, while some Christian missions might not have totally excluded a possibility of preparatory support of colonial aggrandizement, it is wrong to assume that all missions had close connections with colonial politics. Nor was it true that the missions or missionaries could not operate successfully without the support of a colonial government. Klause J. Bade, a noted German theologian, has argued with some exaggeration that the interconnection between missions and colonial policy centred on the question of the need for political stability which was provided either by missions or colonial rule (Bade, 2003:150). Be it the Christian mission or colonial ruler, such view as to who were the first to enter the field may be clarified with S.K. Chaube, who remarks: "to set the record straight, it is necessary to say that it was not the church which enter the hills first. The first to enter the difficult terrains was administration. After the smoothening of the surface by administration, the church went into action and sowed the seeds of progress. A history of the Christian mission in North East India will vindicate this statement" (Chiru, 2007: 105).

When the European colonial forces had established control over non-European countries such as in Asia, Africa, Latin America and Pacific Islands, this consequently provided opportunities for Christian missionaries to follow suit with their missionary adventurism. The basic characteristic of Christianity was its universalism. Religion is an all-pervading supernatural phenomenon in man's life. For this reason, and taking a deep analysis on the nature of its function and approach, Christianity has been perhaps considered as universal. The approach of Christianization earlier was mere on charity and relief, where welfare assistance to groups and individuals includes donations and distribution of materials. The central approach may deemed be fitting to say, as to enhance the livelihoods of such colonialised regions then.

Christianity and colonialism are often closely associated. Of course, the history of colonialism and Christians missions go way back to the fifteenth and sixteenth centuries as result of the expansion of western Europe, the period often referred to as the age of discovery and expansion. Both the colonial powers and mission held the civilizing responsibility which is also known as the "White man's burden" as their shared goal. The mutual binding between missions and colonial politics was at its strongest where the two accepted the 'White man's burden' as a genuine responsibility which some anti-imperialist missionaries referred to as Christian imperialism. During this age of discovery and expansion, as Richard P. Dunn, "the Church sent forth missionaries steeped in European culture that was Christian and Christianity that was intimately bound to European culture" (Dunn, 1909:125). There was no doubt about the close connections between colonialism and Christian missions; they went hand in hand. Their assumption was that nineteenth-century Britain was the ideal paradigm of Christian culture and society. They presumed that God has laid upon Britain the solemn duty of civilizing and Christianising the whole pagan world i.e., the non-Christian world. The motive behind the British administration to invite missionaries was not far to seek—it was primarily for political expediency. This clearly gives the idea of the interrelationship shared by the British colonialists vis-a-vis missionaries. This was, in fact, a critical situation in which many missionaries were placed. Claiming to be both a missionary and a nationalist at the same time, some missionaries even carried with them their national prejudices and took up the work of spreading the gospel as a matter of 'patriotic honour' and 'national duty' (Dena, 1991: 240).

The co-operation between the government and Christian missionaries (mission) existed in the following areas: First, in most cases the missionaries were invited by the British administration to initiate mission works among the people in North East region. Often the missionaries acted as active agents of the colonial empire in various ways during the colonial period. The British colonialists vis-a-vis missionaries benefited from each other's presence in the region. There were difference between them in approach to the tremendous changes taking place in the lives of the people one 'Administered' and the other 'Ministered'. Both agencies were aware that they were bringing about changes in the lives of the people.

As political control advanced, the missionary was prepared to welcome it and to cooperate with the government if he was convinced that its policy was of benefit to the subject people. It should be noted that the missionaries belonged to the epoch of Cecil Rhodes and Bismarck. They were liable to be caught up in the stream of time and semi-consciously to identify their own country's interest with interests of the kingdom of God. No human motives were entirely pure and even the most blameless of missionaries could be victim to this. Instances, though few, showed that some missionaries left the service of their mission and enthusiastically entered into the service of their country in British colonial domain. This inevitably made the missionary appear before the eyes of the world and of the subject peoples in particular the character of agents of their government than as messengers of the gospel. Warneck has justified the missionaries' action that sought to take advantage of the colonial situation. More serious, he had rightly maintained that only the great colonial movements had made the missions acceptable. This proposition is quite dangerous because the white officials' behaviour which was not always in conformity with the Biblical doctrines could stand in the way of the success of missionaries' work, as the native scholar, Prof. Dena argues.

Though in some cases, no doubt that the missionary expansion in various countries was greatly facilitated through its association with the government agencies. For instance, prior to the extension of British political authority into the Igbo country in West Africa, most of the Igbos treated missionary evangelism with respectful indifference. F.K. Ekechi, in this connection has argued that British military imperialism and other forms of colonial exploitation were in fact basic to the decision of many Igbo communities to embrace Christianity. Therefore, some missionaries in West Africa tended to regard British power and prosperity as a blessing for fidelity to the true faith and thus we see nothing insidious about taking advantage of their association with British economic or political expansion to further the kingdom of God (Ekechi, 1971:112). Surely some missionary movements had an almost Hebraic faith. They also believed in worldly success and power which certainly attended the faithful pursuit of duty, and were instrumental in forwarding God's purposes in the world. Where the mission submerged into the colonial plunge without any restrain, its credibility irreparably suffered and it was bound to be, to use Paul Schuetsz' phrase: "the mission is an important factor in culture and civilization." (Chiru, 2007:204).

## Traditional Practices and Western Civilization

Christianity has vast differences with tribal religion and culture. Western anthropologists called this tribal religion as animism. The differences could be in terms of concepts and approaches, origin, composition and functions. Christianity is opposed to almost all the system of animism. However, how the approaches which would work with animistic faith, at the same time to preserve the traditional practices is to be of essence of the missionaries pioneering work. There is no small amount of doubt that would have been forgotten by the preachers whose motto in fact is to preach as it is of the Bible. In most cases this may have been done. The government also did not miss out either. There is non-interference in the animistic way of life was precisely followed for a certain period of time. For instance in Kaikhiu village in Tamenglong district of Manipur where there was conflict between two faiths wherein S.D. Shaw had to abide by the government policy of non-interference in the animistic way of life by ordering the Christians to move to a new village called Sempang without immovable property (Chiru, 2007: 115). The Chirus were covered by proselytization process in this district. The wind from the Eastern direction is always cherished about. The Western wind could be properly studied in line with Hegelian's theory—Western culture i.e., the thesis with Eastern/oriental Tribal communities from the

North East India—anti-thesis. The two need to be viewed so as to reap synthesis. As far as culture is concerned no social reformer wants to completely do away with traditional custom. It would not be wrong to properly preserve all cultural practices as Christ had proved immensely and so by His disciples such as Paul who are both a Jew preserving all Jewish custom and tradition. As rightly Christ pointed out: "I came not to destroy Moses law but to fulfil it" (Matthew: 15:17). In this vein of reasoning Christ ordains tribal society in the North East India. On indigenous culture, Mahatma Gandhi has rightly said, "I do not want my house to be walled on all sides and my windows to be stuffed I want the culture of all the lands to be blown about my houses as freely as possible. But I refused to be blown off my feet by any of them." (Bhave & Krishnan, 1960:85).

In order to preserve and promote the traditional culture and practices, the colonial and independent India promulgated what is called an Inner Line Permit (ILP) since 1873 to protect and promote the culture of the tribals in North East India as elsewhere in the line of Red Indians (USA), Aboriginals (Australia). Recently in India, where permission having taken under protected area permit from the competent authority—Home Ministry, all Indian Mission abroad, FRRCs at Delhi, Kolkata, Chennai, and Mumbai, the Nagaland Government and Home Commissioner and Resident Commissioner of Nagaland Government in India, maximum of 10 days and in a group of four or more persons are exempted for tourist to visit certain parts of Nagaland. However, in the case of married couples, the condition of the minimum number of four would not apply.

## Keen Interest in Backward Tribal Belts

The tribal backward belts can basically be termed regions where a state of barbarism or savagery existed, the pioneer Christian missionaries usually ventured to work in such primitive like backward tribal belts, the North Eastern States of India were no exception. The selfless services which they rendered in terms of their expert knowledge and moral influence tended to have a soothing effect on the people among whom they worked and lived. Looking into the Geographical features of the North Eastern Region of India, it is demarcated with dissected Hilly terrains and Mountainous chains of the Himalayan Ranges. The region is connected to the rest of the mainland India through a narrow stretch of land known as the chicken's Neck or Siliguri Corridor. The region shares international boundaries with five countries which are namely China, Myanmar, Bangladesh, Bhutan and Nepal. The Kingdom of Bhutan lies on the Northern side of the corridor while the countries of Nepal and Bangladesh lies on either side of the corridor. Basically, these geographical features which open a wide door for passage to the neighbouring countries draw the attention of pioneer missionaries in the missionary adventurism in the region. The traditional religion of the indigenous communities in the North Eastern states of India was more of the same, they believe in spirits or souls (animism). Animism was the primitive form of religion. According to E.B. Taylor, evolution of religion has passed through the development process of animism to polytheism and finally to monotheism (Taylor, 1929:424). The conversions of backward tribals for instance, are mainly on the hope of better social life, freedom from caste hierarchies, hoping for better education for children, which helps job prospects, better health care etc. Another reason as to why, these tribals of North Eastern States have seen rapid Christianization could be due to openness of the society and no hard and fast rules to bind them with their freedom of conversion. Donna Strom in her article mentioned about how these animistic religion must have prepared them for Christianity. Unlike Hinduism and Islam, their animism was unorganized and lacked tenacity. The people had no caste system and no written dogmas to hinder them from becoming Christians. Blood sacrifices prepared their minds for the sacrifice of Jesus Christ on the cross (Chiru, 2007:145). Eventually, these converts have declined their participation in traditional religious-cultural celebration.

### Revival or Reconstruction of the Traditional Social Values

According to Raghuvir Sinha, "…Religious aspect is far less important than the social, have not been remodeled on Christian lines, but have been utterly abolished among converts…" (Sinha, 1990:85). Conversion has been the subject of considerable theorizing. It has been defined in terms of ideological, philosophical or other predispositions. Some people see conversion as a consequence of persuasion, as the cognitive act or commitments of a free will, which usually calls for total transformation of one's world-view, value system and behaviour. While some others consider conversion to be miraculous, supernatural events viz., an act of divine 'grace' performed by a single individual person or group of persons, totally transforming or beginning to totally transform the personality (mind, emotion, self-perceptions, etc.) of persons concerned and thereby producing a different understanding of ultimate reality, along with new beliefs, new doctrines, new principles, new behaviours, and new norms of conduct.

From the point of view of the missionaries, conversion is of three kinds: religious, psychological and spiritual. Religious conversion is a process by which one migrates from one religion to another religion, involving merely outward identification with the new religious conversion. It often came upon a person's or person's deep appreciation of the doctrine or teachings of a particular religion by rejecting the other. What was most striking and what the missionary emphatically stressed was the spiritual conversion in which one underwent a mental anguish resulting from conviction of sin and then came to accept Jesus Christ as his Saviour and master.

As this section explores the extent to which their movement is responsible for recovering the lost or abandoned cultural elements for the reformulation or reconstruction of the Tribal Christianity. How far were they willing to incorporate the tribal elements in their system, were they against the beating of drums or dancing or spiritual fervour? According to Rev. R.R. Lolly, "...this dormitory which was considered as their educational institution, the bachelors learnt the art of handicrafts, waging war, social ethics, folk-tales, folk dances and songs... the girls also learn the art of spinning, weaving, embroidery, social etiquette and manners, folk tales and songs" (Chasie, 1999: 56).

These social practices were abolished by the missionaries and were replaced by Christian Youth Clubs, Schools, and Women's Society, festivals like Good Friday, Christmas, and Thanksgiving Day.

But some villages still go along with even after embracing Christianity. The festivals such seed sowing and harvesting, and thanksgiving for the end or planting the crops of the year continue. Therefore, it would be seen still in many Christian tribal of the North-East India that they continue to observe Church Worship Service in which special topics relevant to their church situation are preached, with singing competition of Christian hymns and a special hymn of prayer for the crops for the year and after the worship service other traditional dance and folk songs are displayed. It would be seen here that Jesus Christ is being demonstrated as both the son of man and the son of God (in fact the Bible records more of the son of man). Culturally, a Jew who preserved a Jewish culture, but Paul, who is also a Jew by background tended to say: "...when you are in Rome do as the Romans do...." (I Corinthians 9:20-21). Forgoing discussions witnessed that cultural and religious impingement upon the societies being described for the benefit of the change and continuity of the role Western missionaries imposed on the tribal Christians of the North East India. Other areas which affected change and continuity can also be seen, which are related to human resources development.

Nineteenth century missionaries who established hospitals and schools saw these institutions as aids in saving souls for Christianity. The experience and force of circumstances made the missionaries realize more and more that saving of souls must be accompanied by the saving of physical bodies. Medical work was also one of the most effective means of destroying the traditional world-view and belief system which was essentially super-naturalistic. For instance, the traditional view attributed sickness of misfortunes to malignant and hostile spirits. The village priest was supposed to know which spirit was causing the trouble and what form of sacrifice would appease it. On the contrary, the missionaries were purveyors of the naturalistic world-view as opposed to his super-naturalistic one. In other words, the naturalistic beliefs formed the organizing basis for the missionary's comprehension of the vast majority of day to day events and experience. Of course, the missionary also taught that a supernatural Being created and controlled the universe, but, it was a Copernican universe which he conceptualized, based upon proper training and obtaining the required remedies. The primitive mind in that age could not comprehend that germs caused sickness by moving more or less predictably in humans. With the advance of technology to their own advantage, the missionaries worked with a highly naturalistic view of diseases and medicine which accelerated the breakdown of traditional animistic world-view thereby acting, directly or indirectly, as an effective agent for conversion. Given the basic conceptual difference of disease between naturalistic and super-naturalistic, the role of missionaries in breaking down the traditional resistance to medical aids, by bringing the sick, to hospital and by insisting upon the proper use of prescribed remedies, is to be analyzed while keeping in view how all these helped to facilitate the process of Christianization.

'All missionary movements are guided by certain guidelines and principles. There are examples that pertain to Adinoram Judson who pioneered Burma, convicted by sermons that talked about the love and concern about others. These eventful moments are witness and proof that Christianity is very much part of Indian religious movement. To delineate the issue further one can even go further as was the case of king Xersus rule who expanded his kingdom till India. However, India is a huge country with one billion plus population. So it could have to say that Jesus and His ministry could not have reached every nook and corner of the country. But one thing for sure, Jesus has reached out through His followers to Indians as much as it was done in Middle-east and elsewhere. Therefore, if major religions like Hinduism, Buddhism, Sikhism, Jainism etc. are of Indian origin so is Christianity as much as are the contemporary religions of the first century after the death of Christ. In this context, Christianity which is very much an Indian origin and thus Christianity movement was strongly felt and seriously implanted as Jesus' disciples did visit India and South Africa, and different European countries.

The Western missionaries imbibed these good sacrifices of Jesus. Christ is a rejected messiah, who hailed from Nazareth where it is remarked by Nathanael, one of the other disciples from Nazareth and said, "Can anything good come from Nazareth?" (Johan 1:46). The world came out from nothing (the Bible). All great things or great people come from humble background. India is a great country because of its huge population and its vast size of its territory besides the origin of the world's major religions. On the contrary, poverty is rampant, despite abundant resources. The various civilizations that existed in and around the erstwhile Palestine were of the ones, overall against such tiny baby in the manger to be made a king. Herod killed all babies who were one year and below in search of the baby Jesus who was hidden by the parents from the search of Herod who did not want his kingdom to be succeeded. The Romans held the view that they had no other king than Ceasar Augustus. The general people also felt that Jesus was only for the Jews. The manger represents lowliness and complete contrast of the royal hood. Christ came from splendorous and glittering royal palace as the son of God to be one of the commoners. The son of God learnt and lived as the son of man—born out of the supernatural way of birth that occurred without human sexual relationship. Similarly, missionaries from the West came leaving their countries' better facilities to disease infested terrains in the North East India. The Bible talks about Christ growing in stature and in wisdom. On attaining adulthood, Christ was tortured for being a radical against the Roman authority and Caesar Augustus. For He came to Jews society in the line of David, the king, but Jews rejected Christ, for they considered messiah king to be born was to be from royal hood in all senses. They thought that Christ was apolitical but born a simple carpenter son. In Pilat's judgmental questions Christ repeatedly said that He is the king of the Jews. Pilat was the governor of Judea and was representing Caesar Augustus, and in the Roman world there is no other king than Caesar Augustus. For which Christ was accused and tortured and was at last hanged to death on the cross. Throughout Christ 33 years on earth, forgiveness and love was His prime motto. When Christ was asked about forgiveness, He encouraged forgiving 70 times seven, meaning 7 is the perfect number of the Jews. If a person does wrong and comes for forgiveness, then he is forgiven.

Christ's parable of a good Samaritan, where the fallen Jews was robbed off and beaten black and blue but the two passersby of the fellow Jews crossed the fellow fallen Jew but the Samaritan man came to the rescue of the fallen Jew, which is remarked a proverbial: "The Good Samaritan." As was discussed at length about the Jews and

Samaritans who have nothing to do socially or otherwise. The racial discrimination was at peak in Christ time. He came to the world to do away with such ills of the society till his last breath.

However, Jesus broke all barriers. Indeed, when he was to be born, Luke wrote that: Today in the town of David a saviour was born to you who will be for all the people. The birth of Christ was announced as good news for all the people. Jews waited Messiah to come only for the Jews. But the messiah to come was for the deliverance of captives, to heal the sick and feed the hungry of all dimensions. Above all, Christ came to break the barriers of all castes, class, creed, gender inequality. Jesus appeared to a Samaritan woman in the mid-day noon.

In India caste system has similar story to tell. *Sudras* are cast away from the caste system, where they are ill-treated. Even to the extent that their shadows are shunned as touching of the shadow of low caste is considered polluted and has to undergo cleansing with *puja* or rites. Likewise, the Samaritans and the Jews have the practice that Samaritans hid from the shadow being touched as that would amount to Jews atrocity of the gentile world. That was the reason the Samaritan woman who came to Jacob's well to fetch water at mid-day noon when shadow was the shortest. Christ introduced the concept of one world one family, where there will be no discrimination on the basis of caste, creed, and sex. By status, Jesus is Jew and the Jews have nothing to do with Samaritans. Christ being Jew had limitation to relate with the Samaritans (the Gentile world) and more so women are restricted to openly converse with Jewish man. But Jesus broke such unequal treatment towards women. Therefore, the coming of Christ (being born in lowly status so that Christ ways are humble yet full of power and glory) was a good news for all the people. Jesus came to this world to do away with the conflict and hatred between and among the diverse tribes and communities. When the concept of caste system in India is to be understood, it can easily be most fully understood with the Jews and the Samaritans' relationship that time of more than two thousand years back.

In India religious movements were witnessed with contemporary religions like Buddhism, Jainism, Sikhism and other various Hindu sectarian movements of Rajaram Mohan Roy, Swami Vivekananda, Paramhansa etc. The founding Mauryan Empire, Ashoka, the great, introduced the Buddhist kingdom. He introduced in his kingdom so many non-violent methods of dealing with the neighbouring countries. Non-violence is the method to relate one another among the people between the states, and between the king and the subjects and even with enemies. It was in this regard that Christ is lauded as the champion of peace and non-violence, when Christ was expected a royal birth in a palace, but was given birth in a manger. The manger represents lowliness and complete contrast of the royal hood. Christ came from splendorous and glittering royal palace as the son of God to be one of the commoners. The son of God learnt and lived as the son of man—born out of the supernatural way of birth that occurred without human sexual relationship. The Bible talks about Christ growing in stature and in wisdom. On attaining adulthood, Christ was tortured for being a radical against the Roman authority and Caesar Augustus. For He came to Jews society in the line of David, the king, but Jews rejected Christ, for they considered messiah king to be born was to be from royal hood in all senses. They thought that Christ was a political but born a simple carpenter son.

The racial discrimination was at peak in Christ time. He came to the world to do away with such ills of the society till his last breath. Forgiveness is a way of life for Christ. The Bible reminds that vengeance is mine. God sent His only begotten son not to condemn the world, but to save the world through Him (Bible). When even in the cross, He said: "Father forgive them, for they do not know what they are doing". He forgave even the soldiers who killed Him. God loves the world which is sinful and disobedient. But accept back those who repent and ask forgiveness. This is manifested in the parable of the prodigal son, who left his home taking all his share of wealth and wasted it on wild living but came back to his father and ask for his forgiveness and was accepted by his father. Likewise if we ask Christ for forgiveness He is ever willing to forgive us. Christ motto was forgiveness and establishment of the kingdom of God on earth. When He taught His disciples how to pray "...thy kingdom come, thy will be done on earth as it is in heaven...forgive our debts as we forgive our debtors" (Matthew 6:9-13). There are other avocations of Christ like "if any one strikes on one cheek turn the other". But it is important to note that all these messages of forgiving someone who does wrong against you are not weapon of the weak. It is not submission to someone out of weakness but to forgive someone is work of people with strong will and strong power to forgive others. Therefore, message of forgiveness is the central core to the mission Christ is entrusted with non-violence as the principle that Christ preached to practice. Not to return in the same coin.

Other doctrine that Christ adheres is charity. It is no good to give gifts who are able to return to you. This is something what the one hand gives which the other hand should not know. Giving alms is another universal practice of all faiths. This is done so as to support the poor and the needy. Christ and other founders of faiths like Buddhism, Jainism, Sikhism—the other sectarian Hinduism also have similar doctrine of care and concern for the poor and the needy. The basic difference of Christianity and other faiths is not to retaliate wrong done against you. In Old Testament Moses, the law giver coined through the instruction of God to practice an eye for an eye. Give back with the same coin. If someone does you wrong retaliate it with wrong done in the same coin. However, Christ came with new concept: "Do unto others as you wish to be done by." (Luke 6:31). At the same time, when you do good to others there are chances that there will be bad done to you for doing good to others as was suffered by Christ Himself on the cross for saving souls of sinners from condemnation in eternal hell. God the father in heaven has a reward for such person who laid down life for the sake of others. That objectivity is emphasized to the fullest for human good or what Christ would call it a new humanism. One has to think of others more than selfish thinking for oneself or in other words if any one expects good to be done then he must do first to others. Doing good to others or good works rendered to others is an action. One of Christ's disciples name James emphasized action than faith. Other writers emphasized faith over action. For old Abraham, his only son Isaac was told to be sacrificed, Abraham has faith in God that he would be given another son if he sacrifices to God it is the faith that generates action.

If action is carried without faith in God and injunctions, it can be for conscience. So conscience leading to act good, do good to others can also be from God. All religious faiths can be said to have possessed this inert element called conscience. Even non-Christians but believe in their own deity possesses such conscience. People from other faiths, who are guided by such conscience and doing good works for humanities are entitled God's reward irrespective of which faith or religious doctrine. The commonalities of faith in a sensical world are not only sensically conscious of other faiths and respect for the difference but are very sensitive to other faiths and values embedded in such practical observance of ethical norms and human values.

In India, the intolerance of minorities' faith is alarming issue of religious intolerance and violation of religious rights. Faiths can be challenged as Isaiah did with the worshippers of Baal. The sacrifices made with the similar bulls except without fire, fire that had to consume the bull slaughtered. And that chance was given to the Baal worshippers who failed in the contest. But not with the theory of domination or majoritism, imposition on the minority out of sheer force or discrimination. There are several cases of Christians being attacked for so many decades in India, spanning from the martyrdom of St. Thomas in the 52 AD to Graham Stains with his two sons and beyond cases of Christian atrocities in India in the 21st century. Minority Churches and educational institutions are attacked either for ransom or even rape and arson meted to innocent nuns who sacrifice their lives for the cause of humanity in serving for the development and ennobling cause of enhancing literacy and human index development in India.

The education system in India is sheer colonial hangovers and one likes it or not missionaries from the Christian community carried a yeoman service starting from William Carrey with the Serampore Trio (of which he himself included) to various missionaries, needless to name for want of space. Christian missionaries' educational institutions are living exemplary model of catering and imparting skill-based knowledge to colonies of the imperial countries. William Carey who worked with the mission to establish Baptist mission in upper Assam, prior to abandonment of British Baptist mission field is, 1833 Alexander B. Lish, an Anglo Indian missionary followed by Joshua Roa opened three schools in Chirapunjee.

## Critical Examination in Evangelization of the People of NE India

Ever since the tribal learnt how to read and write it was understood as was essential to fathom the ultimate source of authority and made it as a condition that if an individual had worshipped aright, he must be able to read. So this is how education and evangelism were interlinked. Therefore, the involvement of the missionaries in education programmes was to be viewed as supplementary to the primary task of communicating the 'spiritual' message to the people. Of course, the interest of the colonial officials in such mission's educational programmes was not necessarily religious. It is said that there were presence of both the nature of paternalistic and imperialistic. Colonial masters understood that the education imparted by the missionaries was effective not only in 'civilizing' the natives, but also in making them peaceful and loyal subjects.

Closely intermingling with the main currents of colonial expansion, Western education tended to make colonial occupation appear as beneficial in the eyes of the subject people. The position of the government was, thus, somewhat compromised by the delegation of all educational and other philanthropic works to the Christian missions because the later could undertake such works more cheaply and efficiently than the government could at best effort. In the process, the missionaries were placed almost in the position of the official educationists. They, of course, were subjected to government inspection and such measure of control as might be needed to satisfy government that its money was spent properly. Government on the other hand, explicitly abstained from all interference with religious instruction. Certainly, the government realized that the most effective influence on the subject people must be one that was exercised by such unofficial body to which both the spiritual and the educational works were entrusted. Their strategy was thus to secure the cooperation of missionaries in implementing any measure which they would wish to apply. Inevitably, there would be changes but these changes were to be carefully regulated to suit the interest of government, thereby stabilizing their control over the subject people.

Thus, while the officials looked at introduction of western education as a legitimizing process of colonial rule, the missionaries used it as a vehicle for communicating the Christian message to the subject people. The missionaries considered Sir William Curtis three R's (reading, writing and arithmetic) as the most effective means for winning converts and also for enabling them to learn the basic tenets of the Christian faith. According to them, educational institutions served double purposes: first, as a means of teaching the Christian truth, and secondly, as a means for recruitment or training of future native workers. The early years of the 20th century also marked the beginning of energizing involvement of the native workers, who were trained and recruited in mission stations which inculcated new habits and customs in mass evangelization among their own tribes. The actual evangelization was done better by the cadre groups than the foreign missionaries could hope to do by themselves. This was so because of the realization of the fact that the native workers were more skilled in the use of their own language; they were more fitted to speak in the use of their own language; they were more accustomed to the geography and climate; they were better fitted to speak to their own people about their personal experience; and could live on a very much smaller pay than a missionary from materialistic culture.

One significant development on the non-theological schools was the inclusion of some practical works such as basket weaving and manual work in the curriculum. But the main problem with which the missionaries were confronted was how to make education both practical and spiritual at the same time. This question arose because certain ideas had already laid hold on the native mind, for instance, that education existed to secure a post that should release its holder from manual toil. In order to combat this particular i.e., E.L. Mendus virtually forced his students in Aizawl to work three periods a week at digging a playground out of a hill and also working in the school garden (Rees, 2002: 150-1).

When the Governor of Assam visited the school, he gave some money with a part of which Mendus bought some carpentry tools so as to emphasize the practical side of education and manual work. In all these moves, the basic concept of the missionaries was to fashion the youths—to fashion them in the likeness of Jesus Christ, and the Church by her intercession might discharge education here with a spirit that would make education no longer a menace of a thing to be afraid of but a magnificent interpreter and translator of the truth, and an adornment of the gospel, and an inspiration to labour and service. Thus, the idealization of the goal of education tended to become the spiritualization of education and in this the missionaries failed to achieve a balance between the two.

The practical side of education was perhaps more elaborately stamped on female education to break the great prejudice against girls' education which was very strong amongst the majority of the people. If this was to succeed, it was evident that the school must be made very attractive and at the same time the education imparted must be such as to make the girls an asset in their community. The emphasis on the practical work in female education also aimed at establishing the principle of making some contribution to the cost of girls' education. Therefore, the lady missionaries trained in such arts, formulated the curriculum whereby the girls could give some of their time to work which would be educational and at the same time profitable financially. The practical work which the girls were made to do in addition to their normal subjects included the fellowship which were self-revealing.

## References

Aggarwal, S. Kailash (ed.) (1999). *Dynamics of Identity and Inter-group Relations in North-East India*, Shimla: Indian Institute of Advanced Studies.

Ahmed, Mehtabuddin and Chowdury, Prosenjit (eds.) (1996). *The Turbulent North East*, New Delhi.

Bhattacharyya, N.N. (1995). *Religious Culture of North-Eastern India*, New Delhi: Manohar Publishers & Distributors.

Bhaumik, Subir (1996). *Insurgent Cross Fire: North-East India*, New Delhi: Lancer Publishers.

Bhave, Archarya Vinoba and Krishnan, S. Radha (eds.) (1960). *Mind of Mahatma Gandhi*, Ahemnabad: Navajan Trust.

Bhuyan, Arun Chandan and De, Sibopada (eds.) (1999). *Political History of Assam*, Vol. II 1920-1939, Guwahati: Publication Board Assam.

Bhuyan, Arun Chandan and De, Sibopada, (eds.) (1999). *Political History of Assam*, Vol. I, 1926-1919 Guwahati: Publication Board Assam.

Brajamani, S. (2003). *Economic Growth in Manipur: An Empirical Analysis*, Manipur: S. Romesh Singh.

Brown, R. (2001). *Statistical Account of Manipur*, New Delhi: Mittal Publications.

Chasie, Charles (1999). *The Naga Imbroglio: A Personal Perspective,* Kohima: Standard Printers & Publishers.

Chiru, S.S. (2007). *American Baptist Mission: An Integrating Agent of the Nagas into Indian Union*, New Delhi: Sunrise Publications.

Das, Samir Kumar (1997). *Regionalism in Power*, New Delhi: Omsons Publications.

Dena, Lal (ed.) (1988). *Christian Missions and Colonialism*, Vendrame Institute, Shillong.

Dunn Richard P. and Napoleon's Marshals (1909). Boston: Little Brown & Company.

Ekechi, F.K. (1971). "Colonialism and Christianity in West Africa: The Igbo case", *Journal of Africa History*, 12(1): 103-115.

Ghose, Sumita (ed.) (1998). *Sanjoy's Assam: Diaries and Writings of Sanjoy Ghose*, New Delhi: Penguin Books.

Gohain, U.N. (1942). *Assam under the Ahoms, Guwahati*, Spectrum Publications.

Hazarika, Sanjoy (2000). *Rites Passage: Border Crossings, Imagined Homelands, India's East and Bangladesh*, New Delhi: Penguin Books.

Hudson, T.C. (1911). *The Naga Tribes of Manipur*, New Delhi: Low Price Publications.

Hunter, W.W. (1879). *A Statistical Account of Assam*, Vol. I, Guwahati: Delhi: Spectrum Publications.

Hutton, J.H. (2003). *The Angami Nagas,* Nagaland, Directorate of Art and Culture.

Johnstone, James (2002). *Manipur and the Naga Hills*, New Delhi: Gyan Publishing House.

Kaka, D. Iralu (2000). *Nagaland and India: The Blood and the Tears,* Kohima, Published by Kaka, D. Iralu.

Kamson M. (2004) *A North East Report*, Second Scheduled Areas and Scheduled Tribes Commission Report, New Delhi.

Kumar, B.B. (1995). *Tensions and Conflict in Northeast India*, New Delhi: Cosmo Publications.

Kumar, Nikhilesh (1999). *Survey of Research in Sociology and Social Anthropology in North-East India (1970-1990)*, New Delhi: Regency Publications.

Luthra, P.N. (1974). *Nagaland: From a District to a State*, Shillong: Director of Information and Public Relations.

Maitra, Kiranshankar (2002). *The Noxious Web: Insurgency in the Northeast*, New Delhi: Kanishka Publishers, Distributors.

Mills, J.P. (2003). *The Ao Nagas*, Nagaland: Directorate of Art and Culture.

Namo, Dalle (1987). *The Prisoner from Nagaland*, Nagaland: United Publisher.

Nuh, V.K. (2002). *My Native Country: The Land of the Nagas*, Guwahati: Delhi: Spectrum Publications.

Nuh, V.K. (2002). *The Origin of Naga*, Kohima: Vision Press.

Rees, D. Ben (2002). *Vehicles of Grace and Hope: Welsh Missionaries in India 1800-1970*, London: William Carey Library.

Sachdeva, Rajesh (ed.) (2001). *Language Education in Nagaland: Sociolinguistic Dimensions*, New Delhi: Regency Publications.

Sinha, Raghuvir (1990). *Essay in Social Anthropology*, New Delhi: Concept Publishing House.

Smith, W.C. (2002). *The Ao Naga Tribe of Assam*, New Delhi: Mittal Publications.

Urguhart, David (2015). *The Queen and the Premier*, England: Create Space Publishing.

# 5

# The Tribal Christian of the North East India and their Mission Strategy

The Evangelists had been agitating for long within the Parliament and without for getting full facilities for the missionaries to go to India and spread the Gospel of Christianity among the heathens. While many pleaded for the old policy of non-interference in the religious beliefs of the Indians, the government finally yielded to the pressure of the Evangelists like Wilberforce. As cited elsewhere, the missionaries were permitted by the 1813 Charter Act to promote among the Indian 'useful knowledge and their religious and moral development.' As a result missionary movement entered into a crucial phase spreading even in the far-flung areas of North East India. The first missionaries who surveyed Brahmaputra Valley were Stephen Cacells and J. Gabral, Jesuit missionaries. Basically their tour was to find a route into China and Tibet.

## Early Missionaries in the North East India Amongst the Tribal Communities

In early nineteenth century Serampore mission made a significant contact with the North East India. No doubt, interestingly the initiative for starting missionary enterprise came from government officials. The reason being that what could not be achieved by the military expedition, which produced jealousy and suspicion culminating in endless wars of retaliation and revenge, could be achieved by the power of the gospel. Indeed invitation came from British magistrate of Sylhet to Serampore mission and William Carey sent Krishna Chandra Pal, the first Serampore convert, to Khasi kingdom. Meanwhile, Carey had translation work done with the help of Khasi and in eight months two Khasis and five natives of Assam were baptized.

Baptist Missionary Society (BMS) established Mission Centre at Gauhati in 1829. James Rae was deputed to supervise the newly established Mission Centre. Rae resigned from Superintendent of public works for Assam in the East India Company. He also went for a year's theological training at Serampore. As the going was tough and mission success was not forthcoming even with the help of Ramchandra Nath, a native worker, among the Bengali and Assamese, James Rae was disillusioned. Later Rev. William Robinson tried to rescue Rae from his desperation. However Rae could not reconcile on the failure of his mission. Henceforth, Rae and Robinson abandoned mission and joined government service. Serampore Mission was not disheartened by the failure in the Bramahputra Valley, endeavoured once again to fortify Cheerrapunji Mission. They opened three schools in different places. Unfortunately with the death of Joshua Marshman one of the Serampore trio and the inadequacy of fund, Serampore Mission decided to abandon both the Khasi and the Asian Mission fields. Thus, Serampore mission failure and withdrawal became an opening for Welsh Presbyterean Mission into Khasi field and lower Assam for the American Baptist Mission in 1841 which had already established Mission Centre in upper Assam.

Having opened the way for the mission to evangelize the unruly tribes of Assam, Meghalaya and adjoining areas by the British Agent, David Scott, Nagaland and Manipur fell in the sphere of American Baptist Mission. Having pursued military expeditions and its subsequent failure by the British India, Christian missionaries with genuine interest and intention were determined to undertake the mission of civilizing the unruly and the ignorant Nagas in Nagaland and Manipur. In 1839, the first missionary to pioneer Nagaland at the place called Konyak Naga territory from Sadiya, the outpost in the extreme northern corner of Assam was Rev. Miles Bronson and his wife from the American Baptist Mission.

The prime objective of the American Baptist Mission in India was to open a route to China and Tibet. This interest had been remarkably aroused by the publication of Charles Gutzlaffs 'Journal of Two Voyages along the Coast of China' in 1834. Obviously China Mission was a part of Central Asian strategy and subsequent interest in the North East India was also only an accident or at most a part of this 'Asian strategy'.

This chapter is basically an attempt to find out relatively comparative influence made by the Western missionaries upon the tribal people. It first traces the history of the various church denominations and highlights the paradigm shifts in the history of Christian mission. Pertinent questions such as, are the tribal missions conscious of the culture and various traditional components of the people to whom they claim to evangelize? Are they simply substituting their own ideology and culture to them and neglect to magnify the other culture?

## Colonialism and Christian Missions

In the colonization and imperialism, Christian mission might have had what is called operational unity. But one must not overlook the fact that colonial powers in many cases more or less directly exploited missions for their own ends. In the nineteenth century, the colonialism was coloured with civilizing responsibility and infused the missionaries to take up such challenge. The ideas of advantages of civilisation and its promotion, the concern for progress and development of the natives was incorporated in the agenda of the Berlin Conference in 1885. The Conference started with the evocation ceremonially the omnipotent God. Hence in this Conference both the mission and the colonial politics accepted the 'white man's burden' as a 'genuine responsibility' which some anti-imperialists missionaries referred to as a 'Christian imperialism.' The civilizing mission, they called it in history that having been achieved through this missionary by the colonial India, the tribesmen were reformed and encouraged to abandon de-human living, as a group of untamed people who have their own glory in preserving the age old system of living in their tribal society. But with coming of the Westerners came roads and bridle paths, this in turn attracted trade and commerce. Such accessibility connected the tribesmen to Calcutta and Rangoon. L.W. Shakespeare wrote praiseworthily of the tribesmen of the North East

India, particularly the Nagas. The tribesmen are credited for their skill or indigeniety and not of any much training from the missionaries from the Western society. So were comments from the famous anthropologists like Henry Balfour who wrote about the waning away of the old order of things in the administered area...ornaments which formerly were worn exclusively as insignia of conspicuous prowess and achievement tend to become, under the altered conditions induced by Pax Britannica and government, mere meaningless embellishment of those who have achieved little, or of the merely rich. J.P. Mills abhorred the impositions of foreign culture on the natives' states likewise: "...who puts on foreign clothes adopts with them a foreign outlook. His old environment is no longer good enough for him, and what appears particularly abhorrent to him is the prospect of a lifelong routine of going down a steep hill every morning, doing a day's work in the fields, and coming up a steep hill every evening" (Mills, 1974, 265). The more civilized he is, the less he likes work which entails manual labour...continue the process long enough and you arrive at racial extinction. The missionary is criticized by the colonial writers as representing as 'priest' and at the same time as a 'politician', in fact, in his 'civilizing' aims he creates a market for the traders. He said one of the missionaries actually justified to me (J.P. Mills) the introduction of European clothes on the ground that it was 'good for trade' (Agrawal, 1996:73).

In the case of British control of Assam province free access to Brahmaputra Assam was given to them. This led to the introduction of manufactured goods...brass cooking vessels came to replaced pottery, steel needles to replace wooden or bamboo ones, umbrella to replace palm leaves, kerosene lantern to replace oil reed torches, and white buttons to replace cowry shells. J.P. Mills severely criticized the government officials and the missionaries of encouraging, or at least condoning the tendency to scorn and discard the old dress (Mills, 1974:125). However, the post-colonial World War II has been witnessing a revival of hand-woven dress. In fact, these local products, in the words of Elwin, "Except for a few modern girls, nearly all the women retain much of the hand-woven dress" (Guha, 1996:132). The anthropologist J.P. Mills describes likewise: Men and boys drift in too to pick up odd jobs. The life is regarded as an easy one. There is no daily going to the fields to work. The women, instead of carrying big countless heavy loads of water from springs below the village can draw it from taps. Food and tawry finery be bought. All that is wanted is money, and that they see that men provide. The result is a considerable number, many tribes living without village discipline, and, without religion, animism presupposes a village community to practice it as a whole. Worst still, a younger generation of men and women of every sort of mixture of blood is growing up entirely without tribal or village ties. It is difficult to see any future for them but that of bazaar wasters, who will beget children like themselves. It is the old problem of the de-trivialized natives (Mills, 1974:327).

However, it is observed that in this process of colonialism and Christian mission, educational and medical works were the areas in which missions and colonial structures were most closely integrated and the government offered funds to the missions for theses humanitarian services. They carefully introduced the interest of 'Motherland' in the teaching-learning curricula and in shaping the educational structure. In some cases claiming to be both a missionary and a nationalist at the same time some missionaries even carried with them their national prejudices took up the work of spreading the gospel as a matter of 'patriotic' and 'national duty' as well. Notwithstanding, one thing is quite clear, the basic characteristics of Christianity was 'universalism' as Prof. Lal Dena remarked. The moment it was made to lose its universality by linking it with the colonial interests of a particular country, the mission eventually became colonialism.

However, in most cases, the missionary was far ahead of the government and even of a trade. The missionary usually ventured to work in a backward region where a state of barbarism or savagery existed. The altruistic spirit shown to the native people, the moral influence tended to pave way for political control. Particularly where the missionary and the government belong to the same nationality. Most of the scholars agree that the relation between the Christian missions and colonialism were two movements opposed to each other basically. They were fundamentally driving motivation and inspiration from opposite conceptual extremes. And thus, the interconnection between them was in the nature of highly temporal process which was solely determined by the principle of expediency.

## Origin of Protestant Churches

Jesus is the head of believers in Him called church. He founded the church on the Petra (small rock in which hell cannot prevail over, synonymous to Simon Peter, one of the most influential disciples of Jesus). Jesus chose twelve disciples one of whom called Thomas came to India in 52 AD. He was put to martyr's death at the hand of the Hindu religious group who could not share His conviction, faith, and belief in Jesus (Chiru, 2007). However, the church grew in some parts of south India in course of centuries.

Believers in Jesus often zealous of their faith and conviction entered into conflict with their fellow believers and often failing to reconcile formed various denominational churches, Renaissance in Europe giving the final blow to oneness and unity of the church of Christ by dividing as Roman Catholic and Protestant Churches. Many new Protestant churches formed who opposed the appreciation of the beauties and pleasures of life which resulted in the immoral activities of the church officials. Thus, what is popularly came to be known as Reformation in church history, of which the offshoot came many Protestant churches such as Lutheran, Calvinism, Aana-Baptism, Penticostal, etc. Martin Luther and early Protestant theologians did not share the optimism of the Renaissance, and emphasized human sinfulness in the most uncompromising terms; but by insisting that man could be redeemed only if he felt a sincere faith in Jesus Christ, and that he could not earn salvation simply by obeying the rules prescribed by the Church, they made religion more individualistic (Parkes, 2001). After him was Jean Calvin whose view of the world was extremely gloomy. Denying free will and declaring that all men were 'predestined' either for Heaven or for Hell, he regarded redeeming faith as the free gift of God to those whom he 'elected' for salvation. Like Catholics Lutherarean and Calvinism believed that religious truth should be enforced by the secular authorities. However, some denominations (like Ana-baptist) repudiated all secular authority and looked forward to the rapid approach of the kingdom of God on earth.

As to the research questions such as, is there any will and purpose in their attempt to evangelize or is it just a number games that they played? As per the record of the Christian mission in South Africa by David Livingstone and in the case of Rev Miles Bronson who pioneered the ethnic Naga tribes in the North East India, as in Bronson's case that pioneered the Konyak area in 1839 harvested 37 members on 14 and 15 April, 1867 and it is recorded that 50 Assamese souls were won by 22 missionaries from 1839 to 1867. The mission was never in number game but a genuine soul to win from the headhunting soul at that time, the time-honour practices which were still reported of its practice till 1960s in the case of Livingstone who pioneered the Dark Continent was no doubt an ardent missionary and a medical doctor who desired no large church of nominal adherents which can be witnessed in his own writings which said: "Nothing will induce me to form an impure church. Fifty added to the church sounds fine at home, but if only five of these are genuine what will it profit in the Great Day?" (Livingstone, 2015: 316). He was a lover of thorough finished work who allowed no celebration of Lord's Supper because he did not deem the professing Christians believing consistent lives. From these two instances of missionization cited, one in Africa and similar one in Assam province of erstwhile British colony, representing a strategy of Christian mission revealed that the number game seemed to be misnomer. Thus this chapter critically examine tribal Christianity and see that whether or not they are finally free from Western Christianity or they are still hands and glove in tune with them after all these years.

The impact of Western Christianity upon the tribal of the North East India is enormous in terms of human resources development which includes primarily education, healthcare and other developmental parameters index. Christianity in the North East dates back to late 1820s and 1830s depending on a specific North East ethnic concentration as of that time in Assam province of erstwhile colonial India. When the Western missionary landed in the North

East India, the first thing done by the mission is to educate or train in the education of Western culture of course not neglecting completely the tradition and cultural practices of the ethnic tribes. Schools and hospitals play an important role in civilizing the tribesmen in the North East India. Education was planted in the tribal world of the North East India with the mind to educate the otherwise hidden world of the frontier India. Education in India of Macaulay was to create cheap *babus* to serve the colonial English imperialist purpose of administration in India. Education policy was formulated in such a way that upper caste of the Indian society was made exclusively accessible to the then education so as to have trickle-down effect to the lower castes Indian society. However, since there is no caste system applicable save in certain pockets like Tripura, Manipur but the rest of the present states have the tribal domination and in such cases caste system is not applicable. However, to say nil prevalence of the sociological social stratification in a given society is also an academic ignorance. So it is presumed that in some form of high and low class if not caste is there in overall North East Indian society. Sociologically caste is a closed system and class is an open system. In the area of administration and customary practices and its impact of the Western culture upon tribal society is the issue that no scholar can afford to maintain that change was not there. The agent or instrument of change were identified in the form of missionaries and the introduction of formal educational and medical or forms of institutions. Maybe in informal education was conducted in the bachelor's dormitory. Training in such informal education in the colonial times included traditional handicrafts and skills related to man. However, in some cases such informal education was also conducted for the girls who attained the puberty age. The girls mostly learned skills related to women such as making looms for weaving etc. These informal schools of traditional customary practices in characteristic were modified to formal schooling by the missionaries. Continuation of these traditional practices in certain ethnic society was witnessed in the village authority courts in the post-colonial era. But in most cases, the practice of bachelor's dormitory education of traditional values and practices were slowly being eliminated and got replaced by Western educational institutions called school. Traditional courts of pristine in nature got slowly diminished its presence felt with colonial judicial system but with modified version even to this day. Traditional belief system got replaced by Christian belief system. No one can claim that traditional belief system has no meanings in that point of time except renaissance either from Europe or later in India in 18th century brought changes as enlightened belief system coupled with protestant reformation and capitalist economic system in the otherwise socialistic pattern of economy in the ethnic tribes of the North East India. In the post-colonial era, or rather with the liberation of India from the British yoke officially in 1947, many of the ethnic tribes from the North East India either declared ahead of Indian independence, as in the case of Naga ethnic tribes who claimed independence in 1946 and subsequent 1951 plebiscite for full sovereign country. Many other ethnic tribes in the North East India demanded various administrative mechanisms from India. These demands included are the ethnic tribe like Mizos, Hmars, Kuki-Chin, Bodo so on and so forth. As to the enlightenment of the natives like any Renaissance movement, particularly of Indian context where few Indians got the opportunity to get trained or imparted of Western education who later served for the Indian independence movement and got liberated from the British yoke on 15 August, 1947.

The general base year of advent is 1830s in Christian mission in North East India. And standing in its own feet, which may be termed nationalization of local leadership (1950s but in many other sectarian denominations they might not have existed by then in North East India at least) by the Christian mission of different denominations could be put on record as 1900 with formation of the Associations etc. As most of the mission stations of Christianity in North East India by the second or third quarter of the twentieth century had developed a kind of preparation for national leadership and self-reliance which was achieved in the mid-fifties of the twentieth century.

It will outline how mission work started within the various churches and examine exactly what were the aims and objectives of doing mission among the other people. It also shows factors that motivated the 'tribal' for this task and how they met the financial needs for this purpose. It will also analyze the mission of the larger denomination among the North East Christianity from the perspective of a post-colonial approach. Are the tribal Christians really doing and starting a mission of their own? Are their strategy and plan an outcome of their own imagination and from the own mentality or from the study of the Bible? Or is it just a replica of the 'mother' Western missionaries, who had coop them up so much that they cannot think for themselves till now?

The North Eastern Tribal Christians as discussed elsewhere that certain traditions and customs of the tribals from the North East Indian remained intact. As to the question that of self-finance and standing on their own feet issues can be understood particularly with certain denominations. For instance in the case of American Baptist mission which is self-finance so to say in terms of support and administration, could stand on its feet by 1950s. The last missionary of foreign origin was Rev. Michael Scot and thus did pave the way for the national/native leaders to take over leadership full in charge in the state of Manipur and Nagaland in addition to other North East Indian states. American Baptist Mission has to do with Naga Tribal a lot as missionary was said to be brain behind in the case of Naga nationalism politically. He was accused of internalization of the Naga cause in the United Nations. Other missionaries like Lorrain and Savidge who pioneered Mizoram with Welsh mission and expanded to southern Manipur, had similar story to tell about its nationalization of leadership in the hand of the natives. There were various other sectarian denominations including Roman Catholics, Seventh Day Adventists, Jehovah Witness, Evangelicals, Methodists, Independent Churches, Pentecostal/Assemblies of God etc. The above base year as 1900 is determined as by then most of the Christian missions after Charter Act of 1813 declaration was made for introduction of Christian mission in the Indian sub-continent. In the North East India, 1830s was the year Nagaland and Mizoram including neighbouring areas were established of its mission stations. However, 1900 as base year being set only because many mission stations by different Christian denominations had different institutions already established certain nascent educational and medical infrastructure in their own mission stations. Through such mission institutions converts were reaped as part of the strategy. The initial strategy of the missionisation is contextualization. In this involved mastering the local language. Most of the mission stations and the missions first learn the local languages.

As most of the Christian missions became more firmly established, the evangelizing responsibilities were handed over to the medical groups with long-term goal of creating self-supporting and self-governing indigenous churches. It is observed that indigenous churches were theoretically to be independent of mission both in the matter of control and support. But in reality, the foreign missionaries continued to exercise paternalistic control over the development of churches and the evangelistic works in particular. This was inevitable because as a rule the native workers have more trust in Western missionaries than in the native themselves. The missionaries also looked upon these native people as 'sheep' who needed the 'Western shepherd'. Naturally, there was a general concern for orientation of the evangelists and pastors who were required sometimes to do refresher courses at mission stations. They were not only with the missionaries in school hours, but were their constant friends and companions in their leisure too. The steady growth and development of the embryonic indigenous church was due to keen evangelistic zeal of these workers. Having thus prepared the native workers for the initial task of self-propagating programme, the missionaries began to think in terms of proper channelization of the zeal for evangelization to other secular works. Because they realized the fact that they had, growing under their hands, an indigenous church that was creating demand for education in order to safeguard its own existence, for better food and economic conditions to sustain the new sense of the value of human life; for better social conditions; for sanitation and more hygienic personal habits. Feeling also the impact of nationalist movement in the country, the missionaries thought that it would be a healthy move in bringing a clear relationship between the foreign mission and the indigenous churches. Keeping this object in view, the missionaries adopted a gradualistic approach to give frank and cordial recognition to the indigenous churches life and leadership in all efforts for evangelizing and participating in the policy-making process.

Basically, the missions entered into a policy of cooperation with the state just to safeguard their monopolistic control over education. Once this was threatened, they preferred to delink their dependence upon the state grant or financial assistance. But in Manipur, the situation was reversed when J. Shakespeare, who was known for his pro-mission attitude, took over the Political Agency. With his help and encouragement, village schools were re-organised on three years basis in about a dozen villages in tribal Christian areas like Ukhrul. These schools were run by newly recruited young men from the earlier school, whose salaries were paid by the state. Along with this scheme, another important arrangement was made with the political Agent, viz., the bringing in to the central (station) school (at Ukhrul) two boys from each village where no village school had been established. They were to have three years course, with the provision that if they were inclined to remain on for further study, they could do so, and also the boys, from village schools who desired further knowledge would be allowed after their three years course to attend this central school. The station school and the church records show that quite 95 per cent of the scholars who had passed through this school for either short or long periods had become Christians. Rev. Pettigrew felt that this effort was amply rewarded. From here the first Kuki missionary was harvested. And so were many other ethnic communities at least from the point of American Baptist Mission as an oldest Christian mission in the North East India.

## The Impact: Systematically de-cultured and Simultaneously Indoctrinated

As was witnessed in many societies around the globe, the coming in of the British colonial masters and missionaries in the nineteenth century had great setbacks on the diverse ethno-cultural practices and to the varied ecclesiastical traditions of the region; it has deep rooted impacts in areas of political, social, economic and religious factors. Politically, it brought a wider nation-state political dimension which led to the dilution of traditional customary laws and norms.

The entire nineteenth-century, especially the second half of it was a period of cultural and religious ferment in India under the influence of Western culture and missions. The British administration justified their encouragement and funding of the Christian missions on the grounds that the hill people did not have any religion. When the tribes had been pacified through the use of military force, the missionary education system was simply a convenient and cheap way of rendering a service that would otherwise have been the responsibility of the government (Downs, 2003:172)

By inculcating modern education in schools the missionaries worked toward changing the habits and lifestyles of the indigenous peoples of the region. The missionaries insisted that, if one became a Christian one should not participate in Hindu festivals or worship other gods. These converts who were associated with the missionaries who live with them, were rather governed by the missionaries vis-a-vis colonialist, they were taught the art of keeping their surroundings clean, to put-on good clothings, and the scenario of these locals being governed by the missionaries in their walks of lives itself is imperialism in nature. Though there are opinions different from the above stated lines, group of scholars of which F.S. Downs and Milton Sangma are representative argue that the missionaries were not guilty of colonial engagement because they had their own goals and objectives and these were quite different from those of the colonial British administration. Sometimes, certain Christian families stop contributing or participating in tribal festivals. This creates fraction at village and family levels. Missionaries through their proselytizing activities succeeded in converting one or two members of a family. It is alleged that missionaries through these converted members try to influence other members of the family. This creates tension within families which often accentuates communal rivalry. To be a true convert basically meant to shun all traditional beliefs, faith and worship, eventually discovering a new "You". Clark moved to Ao-land in 1876 and started evangelization through preaching, schools, and literature work. Godhula, who was the real pioneer among the Ao-Naga converts, was given the "Christian" name of Rufus Brown. Edward Winter Clark and his wife, Mary Mead Clark, have been associated with the pioneering endeavour among the Ao-Nagas, Godhula, was also being referred to as Clark's assistant (Puthenpurakal, 1986:273).

Ashis Nandy asserts that the colonization of the mind is no less debilitating a form of colonization than the material/geographical form. He offers this succinct summary of the psychological impact of such colonization: "This colonialism colonizes minds in addition to bodies and it releases forces within the colonized societies to alter their cultural priorities once for all. In the process, it helps the concept of the modern West from a geographical and temporal entity to a psychological category. The West is now everywhere, within the West and outside; in structures and in minds" (Nandy, 1983:49).

There are many Johns, Josephs and Matthews etc. in the present society, this probably is one result of westernisation in the mindset of the younger generations, and childrens of the present generation are more inclined towards westernised culture. People often give themselves names foreign to their wisdom and practice, the traditional way of naming a new born child, taking half the names of their grandparents which is seen in the Chin-Kuki-Zo communities with its uniqueness. This practice of naming a new born child has lost its genuineness, as the modern families were more inclined towards western Names, the culture of adding a Christian name along with their ancestral names has become most acceptable trend now. At an instance, children were taught to abandon their traditional hairstyles and to adopt the style of the English and the missionaries. The motive behind Christianization on the other hand was of social and administrative purpose—the British saw an opportunity to extend its administration that would minimize greatly the state's treasury working through the missionaries among the native people. "Every single aboriginal child would be removed from his/her home, family, community and culture at the earliest possible age and held for years in state sponsored 'educational' facilities, systematically de-cultured, and simultaneously indoctrinated" (Downs, 2003:68).

The Zeliangrong Heraka Movement spearheaded by Haipou Jadonang, a Rongmei, Naga spiritualists which was later succeeded by his cousin Rani Gaidinliu after he was hanged by the British in

1931, was based purely in preserving the Zeliangrong culture and traditions. It is often described as a reform movement, a revival of the Naga tribal religion. The Zeliangrongs are one of the communities who uphold the valour and virtues of their great Naga forefathers, the idea of Heraka is centred to the worship of God Tingwang only, this angered British rulers and foreign Christian missionaries. Zeliangrong Heraka Association (ZHA) believes that "Loss of religion is loss of culture and loss of culture is loss of identity" (N.C. Zeliang, 2005). Genuine cultural identity of any society is comprised of indigenous religion, native culture, language, glorious history of forefathers, art and crafts, rites and rituals, traditional village institutions and customary laws (N.C. Zeliang, 2005). There were even instances of English missionaries vehemently opposing efforts by Indian Christian leaders to form indigenous missions. This showed that even missionaries were not free from racism. Westernisation is so much deep rooted in the present society that the concept of joint families is fastly decreasing everyone wants to remain aloof from others. Marriages are rapidly breaking; it has eventually given rise to single families.

It has been often argued that European medicines and hospitals were instrumental in saving lives and improving the living qualities of the people. What is never acknowledged is the displacement of traditional indigenous medicines and medicine persons and the cultural role these played. According to Michael Mann, "Colonial medicine was also considered a useful tool for ruling the country in its potential for colonizing and civilizing the bodies of the people. The impact is so deep rooted that the indigenous tribals are socially and culturally assimilated with Western world." (Tine & Mann, 2004:4)

The advent of colonialism; say British rule in the North East India has witnessed drastic changes in the lives of the indigenous tribes of the region, when these primitive like society consisting of several clannish division and diverse ethnic communities were exposed to Christianity, significant numbers have embraced the faith. The question of religious conversion often occupies central stage in politics. Faith in God and adherence to a particular religion is a matter of conscience and a subject of individual freedom. Change of faith and informed choice are constitutional rights that guarantee personal choice. James Johnstone, the then political agent of Manipur, however regarded Christianization of the people as the only effective means for mutually attaching them to the government (Allen, 1905:75). The Tribals of the North Eastern States for the most part have no written history, they greatly depend on oral traditions as such their folklores, cultures and traditions are passed on through generations. The contribution of Western missionaries avis-a-vis British colonialist in the promotion of Western education and the compilation of their histories, literatures of these primitive and backward tribals of these regions during the British rule in India are the works of the Westerners, they have attributed so much that their works and contributions in such fields have been considered of immensely important for scholars and research works in the present generation, without which such works shall possess no authenticity. They are to this day lauded for their "accomplishments" in education. The tribals or say the indigenous peoples of these region rely heavily on arts and culture, folk songs, dances, legends and stories. The missionaries were responsible for the introduction of modern education, literacy and literature to the native people whose own learning system and means for the transmission of knowledge were oral. The missionaries were responsible for reducing what were life-giving oral traditions down to stagnant written languages. Critical scholars were of the opinion that, beneath much of the old testaments there remained a residue of older tradition which had originated in folklores. In other words, God himself encountered his people, the Israelites through their folk culture. In the pages of the Bible, one can find folk features and cultures. When the evangelist Matthew, wanted to tell us who Jesus is, he started by listing long list of genealogy, tribals would understand the logic of Matthew. We may also say, in folklore and cultures, the tribals are ultimately tied to their lands.

Christianity is a very community oriented religion much in harmony with tribal outlook and mentality in general. Christianity is also a religion of personal discipleship and loyalty to Christ. This is evident in the celebrations. The value implies in the sharing of one's wealth in a conspicuous gospel values. It would be in our wisest act to enlighten our children about their roots, about their rich cultural heritage and to not be engulfing with the rapid globalisation.

## Conclusion

To sum up in the capsule form, conclusive statements can be made as:

1. The prime objective of the American Baptist Mission (the oldest Christian mission in the North East India) in India as it was stated was to open a route to China and Tibet.

2. This interest had been remarkably aroused by the publication of Charles Gutzlaffs 'Journal of Two Voyages along the Coast of China' in 1834. Obviously China Mission was a part of Central Asian strategy and subsequent interest in the North East India was also only as having opened the way for the mission to evangelize the unruly tribes of Assam, Meghalaya and adjoining areas by the British Agent, David Scott, Nagaland and Manipur which fell in the sphere of American Baptist Mission.

3. Having pursued military expeditions and its subsequent failure by the British India, Christian missionaries with genuine interest and intention were determined to undertake the mission of civilizing the unruly and the ignorant Nagas in Nagaland and Manipur where in 1839 the first missionary to pioneer Nagaland at the place called Konyak Naga territory from Sadiya, the outpost in the extreme northern corner of Assam was Rev. Miles Bronson and his wife from the American Baptist Mission.

4. In the nineteenth century, the colonialism was coloured with 'civilising responsibility' and infused the missionaries to take up such challenge. The ideas of advantages of civilisation and its promotion, the concern for progress and development of the natives was incorporated in the agenda of the Berlin Conference in 1885. The Conference started with the evocation ceremonially the omnipotent God. Hence in this Conference both the mission and the colonial politics accepted the 'white man's burden' as a genuine responsibility

which some anti-imperialists missionaries referred to as a 'Christian imperialism.' The civilizing mission, they called it in history that having been achieved through this missionary by the colonial India, the tribesmen were reformed and encouraged to abandon de-human living, as a group of untamed people who have their own glory in preserving the age old system of living in their tribal society.

5. As per the record of the Christian mission in South Africa by David Livingstone and in the case of Rev Miles Bronson who pioneered the ethnic Naga tribes in the North East India, the number game seemed to be misnomer as it can be seen that the Konyak area in 1839 harvested 37 members on 14 and 15 April, 1867 and it is recoded that 50 Assamese souls were won by 22 missionaries from 1839 to 1867. The mission was never in number game but a genuine soul to win from the headhunting soul at that time, the time-honour practices which were still reported of its practice till 1960s. Livingstone who pioneered the Dark Continent was no doubt an ardent missionary and a medical doctor who desired no large church of nominal adherents.

6. The impact of Western Christianity upon the tribal of the North East India is enormous in terms of human resources development which includes primarily education, healthcare and other developmental parameters index. Christianity in the North East dates back to late 1820s and 1830s depending on a specific North East ethnic concentration as of that time in Assam province of erstwhile colonial India. When the Western missionary landed in the North East India, the first thing done by the mission is to educate or train in the education of Western culture of course not neglecting completely the tradition and cultural practices of the ethnic tribes.

7. Education policy was formulated in such a way that upper caste of the Indian society was made exclusively accessible to the then education so as to have trickle-down effect to the lower castes Indian society. However, since there is no caste system applicable save in certain pockets like Tripura, Manipur but the rest of the present states have the tribal domination and in such cases caste system is not applicable. However, to say nil prevalence of the sociological social stratification in a given society is also an academic ignorance.

So it is presumed that in some form of high and low class if not caste is there in overall North East Indian society. The agent or instrument of change were identified in the form of missionaries and the introduction of formal educational and medical or forms of institutions.

8. As to the question that of self-finance and standing on their own feet issues, it can be understood particularly with certain denominations as is the case, for instance, American Baptist mission which is self-finance so to say in terms of support and administration, could stand on its feet by 1950s. There were various other sectarian denominations including Roman Catholics, Seventh Day Adventists, Jehovah Witness, Evangelicals, Methodists, Independent Churches, Pentecostal/Assemblies of God etc. In the North East India, 1830s was the year Nagaland and Mizoram including neighbouring areas were established of its mission stations. However, 1900 as base year being set only because many mission stations by different Christian denominations had different institutions already established certain nascent educational and medical infrastructure in their own mission stations.

9. In the colonization and imperialism, Christian mission might have had what is called operational unity. But one must not overlook the fact that colonial powers in many cases more or less directly exploited missions for their own ends. In the nineteenth century, the colonialism was coloured with 'civilizing responsibility' and infused the missionaries to take up such challenge. Most of the scholars agree that the relation between the Christian missions and colonialism were two movements opposed to each other basically. They were fundamentally driving motivation and inspiration from opposite conceptual extremes. And thus, the interconnection between them was in the nature of highly temporal process which was solely determined by the principle of expediency. The school masters were not ready to cooperate when the situation forced the Christian mission in their zeal for saving souls rather than carrying the colonial responsibility. Also one must never forget that missionaries were ahead of the groundwork for administration (Colonial India) not *vice versa*.

## References

Agrawal, M.M. (1996). *Ethnicity, Culture and Nationalism in N.E. India*, New Delhi: Indus Publishing Company.

Allen, B.C. (1905). *Gazetteer of Naga Hills and Manipur*, New Delhi: Mittal Publications.

Chiru, S.S. (2007). *American Baptist Mission: An Integrating Agent of the Nagas into Indian Union*, New Delhi: Sunrise Publications.

Downs, S. Fredericks (2003). *History of Christianity in India*, Vol. V, Part 5, Bangalore.

Guha, Ramchandra (1996). "Savaging the Civilised: Verrier Elwin and Tribal Question in Late Colonial India", *Economic and Political Weekly*, Vol. XX1, Nos. 35, 36, and 37 Special Number.

Harald, Fisher Tine and Michael, Mann (2004). *Colonialism as Civilizing Mission*, London: Wimbledon Publishing Company.

Lal, Dena (ed.) (1988). *Christian Missions and Colonialism*, Vendrame Institute, Shillong.

Livingstone, David (2015). *Missionary Travel and Research in South Africa*, Edinburgh: Create Space Independent Publishing Plate form.

Mills, J.P. (1974). *Ao Nagas*, England: Oxford University Press.

Nandy, Ashis (1983). *The Intimate Enemy: Loss and Recovery of Self under Colonialism*, England: Oxford University Press.

Nari, Rustomji (ed.) (1989). *Verrier Elwin: Philanthropologist Selected Writings*, New Delhi: Oxford University Press & North Eastern Hill University.

North East India : A Bibliography (2002). New Delhi: Nehru Memorial Museum and Library.

Puthenpurakal, J. (eds.) (1996). *Impact of Christianity on North East India*. Shillong: Vendrame Institute Publication.

Thomas, C. Joshua and Das, Gurudas (2002). *Dimensions of Development in Nagaland*, New Delhi: Regency Publications.

Zeliang, N.C. (2005). Zeliangrong Heraka Association, April 10.

# 6 Formulation of Mutual Co-existence: Cultural Response to Westernization

## Theorizing the Theories

Sociologists theorize sociological theories embedded in a particular social context. Such context deeply influence the individual/ society. Each sociological thinker or theorist has to respond to the social situation in which he or she exists and try to make sense of the enveloping culture. That is to say that sociological theory is the sociologist's response to the context in which he lives and works. As is well known sociology developed first in the West that it percolated to India in the 20th century. The French Revolution in 1789 created such an urgent context that it became an important element to create a need for sociological theorising. Thus, the French Revolution gave rise to many changes in that society. These changes were beneficial in the main but these were also problematic. One of these problems was the law and order maintenance in France. Some thinkers even advocated that law and order in France after the revolution was worse than what existed in the Medieval Ages. Not surprisingly the major theorists like Comte and Durkheim were deeply concerned with law and order.

Basically there are three sociological theories: the symbolic interactionist perspective, the functionalist perspective, and the conflict perspective. These perspectives offer sociologists theoretical paradigms for explaining how society influences people, and *vice versa*. Each perspective uniquely conceptualizes society, social forces, and human behaviour. The intention here is to find out the relevance of these theories along with missiological and hermeneutics approaches including post-colonial debates of various post-colonial religious approaches like a theistic approach, an unknown god approach, an inclusive approach, a fulfilment approach and a henotheistic approach would be an accomplishment in itself.

The term "theory" has a broad and a narrow meaning. In the broad sense missiological theory might mean systematic statements of truth or the beliefs and knowledge in missiology as a field. David Bosch points out in his magisterial treatment, *The Theology of Mission*, that in addition to truth (theory) and justice (praxis); people also need beauty or the "rich resources of symbol, piety, worship, love, awe, and mystery." (Bosch, 2005:431) He is using theory in the broad sense. However, the study here is proposed making use of a narrower definition of theory. It may seem pretentious since missiology and even the social sciences are not the same as the natural sciences that use the narrower definition, but believe that using the narrower definition of theory can make a contribution to developing missiological theory. One of the crucial aspects of post-colonial debates is the constant move between the past and the present: In missiological terms, post-colonial theory does not only reveal the complicity of the Christian missionary enterprise with the structures of colonial oppression but stresses the necessity of acknowledging this complicity for the sake of a renewal of creation according to the promise of God's reign.

By bringing to light the unequal process of representation through which the historical experiences of the once-colonised have been framed by the West, and the intertwined histories of the coloniser and the colonised, a post-colonial discourse takes us beyond simplifications, essentialisms and dichotomies. We could also say, post-colonial theory and hermeneutics confronts theologians with two sides of the proverbial coin: Difficulty of overcoming these differences and divides, in terms of the stark realities of a post-colonial world which is neocolonialist, imperialist, and capitalist in terms of a globalised political economy.

In the context of the tribals of the North East India, despite exemption from the Indian Special Economic Zone which is opposed tooth and nail in other tribal belts in India, the differences in custom and tradition are creation of God as no one zebra lines are same from the other zebra. Every community has its own charm and ills of its own. The creation of the Second World War is enormous which is hugely contributed by Woodrow Wilson with his famous Fourteen-Point Declaration from which United Nations and its many conventions are enshrined especially for the colonized and the marginalized Third World countries. Despite all these declarations for world peace and order which can never be realized in true sense of the term. For haves and have-nots differences and inequalities remain the order of the world rather than Justice and peaceful co-existence and harmony. The reason is not good UN Declarations but no good implementations. Can the Americans think of less privileged nations by cutting their expenses? The Pope has rightly said that those rich capitalists were not sharing their riches and wealth was stealing from the poor (Haislmaier, 1984, 21).

These are exacerbated with the points raised since its origin some 25 years ago, post-colonial critics have grappled with the ambivalent notion of difference and have paid special attention to the hurtful memories of those whose lives have been marginalized and oppressed by the despoilment of their cultures, desecration of their sacred places, and in some cases even by the use of economic and military power to ensure the numerical growth of the Christian community.

A post-colonial study has gained more importance also in theology because post-colonial critique allows for a wide-ranging investigation into power relations in various contexts. "The post-colonial consequently requires an ethical commitment to, and identification with, those struggling under global structures of domination and exploitation. It is a search for a just form of international relations" (Dube, 2002:102).

With overlapping positions as post-colonial subjects, in the words of Letty Russell, "...to be post-colonial subjects is to recognize that we are all in this predicament of a groaning and unjust world together and that often we are both colonizer and colonized at the same time" (Russel, 1974:101). Or, in other words, we are the other and marginalized. At the same time, some of us, to a greater or lesser extent, are the beneficiaries of power and privilege in terms of race, class, nationality, and education. We straddle the divides between outsider and insider, grappling with the conflicts and contradictions of being part of a post-colonial world formed by inequalities and domination.

But we forget that we are commissioned "to be reconciling and healing agents by resolving conflicts, bringing peace with justice (praxis), comforting and empowering people excluded from belonging to families and civil societies, caring for the environment and restoring people to physical and psychological well-being" (Downs, 2003:57). Thus, who are insider-outsiders searching for ways of dealing with the other in a hospitable and relational manner and thus overcoming the dichotomies between self and other in creative new ways? But, caring for the environment is entrusted in Christendom as part of the creation theory which some theorists have manipulated to serve the vested interest. Christology facilitates Paul's ecological concern on eco-justice which involves the well-being of humans and of nature. Human activities over two centuries committed drastic ecological and climate change. The Christian response to ecological crises would involve traversing the path that the missionaries traversed (Fernandes, 1998). They contributed in discoveries of the old value of the culture of dominant classes amongst the colonized people and renewed the planet rediscovering the value system of the ecosystem people. Although Christian's engagement with the environment is of long history yet they are blamed for their lukewarm attitude towards environmental concern (White, 1967). For evangelism pre-dominates care for environmental concern. The post-modern theory calls for careful study that pertains to ecological crisis. Creation theory needs special revisit for ecological concern. For God created man in His own image and has responsibility to relate with God and nature. Therefore, this needs reinterpretation to correct the misinterpretation of 'over dominance' that contributed in exploitation of man upon nature.

St. Paul describes the groaning of creation anxiously waiting for liberation/salvation and healing (Romans 8:19-22). Charles Birch pointed out: "An ecological sustainable earth is a necessary requirement for distributive justice. There is no possibility of justice in a world in which the rich exploit resources at the expenses of the poor and of other life" (Granberg, 1984). This echoes what in fact, the human relationship with one another, particularly managing economic resources is an important aspect of ecology Thus, some of the causes of the ecological crisis are development, modernization, and industrialization. However, these are again needed with the changes of time and people. All these developments have least to do with the crisis directly but supporters of theistic evolution generally harmonize evolutionary thought with belief in God, rejecting the conflict thesis regarding the relationship between religion and science—they hold that religious teachings about creation and scientific theories of evolution need not contradict each other. It covers a wide range of beliefs about the extent of any intervention by God, with some approaching deism in rejecting the concept of continued intervention. For a theist (a Christian, Jew, or Moslem), natural does not mean "without God" because we believe that God initially designed nature, then created nature and now constantly sustains nature, and can guide nature (in a natural-appearing way that blends smoothly with the normal operation of nature) so one natural result occurs instead of another natural result.

Another approach is an unknown god approach referred here is based on (New Testament Bible) Acts chapter 17 with a number of historical documents and sources linked to the sixth century before Christ, the city of Athens being devastated and decimated by a mysterious plague. When no explanation for the plague could be found, and no cure was in sight, the approach was to assume that one of the city's many gods had been offended. When all efforts failed to discern which god had been offended, and which had brought the plague upon the city, an outside consultant was brought in from the Island of Cyprus, whose name was Epimenides. Epimenides concluded that it was none of the known gods of Athens which had been offended, but some, as yet, unknown god. He proposed a course of action which, if it worked, would at least provide a possible remedy for the plague. He had a flock of choice sheep, of various colours, kept from food until they were hungry. On the given day, he had these sheep turned loose on Mars Hill, on what was a very succulent pasture. For any sheep not to have eaten his fill would have been unexplainable. He had the sheep turned loose and watched carefully, to see if any sheep would lie down and not eat, even though hungry and in prime grazing. Several sheep, to the amazement of those watching, did lie down. Altars were erected at each spot where a sheep lay down, dedicated to an "unknown god." On those altars, the sheep which lay in that spot was sacrificed. Almost immediately, we are told, the plague began to subside.

The leaders of the city sought to determine which of the gods it was and then determine a way of appeasing that god. This was no easy task, since the city of Athens had literally hundreds of gods, which is referred to as the god capital of the world, a place so full of gods that the Athenians "must have needed something equivalent to the Yellow Pages just to keep tabs on the many deities already represented in their city" (Hum, 1998, 55).

Another theory is Henotheist theology which has historical roots in Ancient Egyptian religion, Pagan Hermetism and Hermeticism. Today, it is at work in the East in Brahmanism (Hinduism) or in Taoism and is part of the Western Mystery Tradition.

The firstness of the Divine is not in conflict with this diversity. The sole God is not against the other Deities, but Self-manifests as Divine Names, Attributes, Presences, Hierarchies, Gods and Goddesses, etc. Such a bi-polar concept of the Divine does not eliminate the notion of firstness, for in the hierarchy of Divine Names, "I" or "I AM" remains the "summum bonum" (cf. the Decad of the Pythagoreans, or "Kether", the "Crown" in Qabalah).

Historically, distinction is made between four theo-ontological models of the Divine:

*Semitic model*: God is One and Alone. He, the sole God, is an unknown and unknowable Divine Person, Who wills good and evil alike (cf. Judaism & Islam).

*Greek model*: God is a Principle of principles, the best of the best (Plato), the unmoved mover (Aristotle), the One even ecstasy does not reveal, impersonal and in no way evil or tainted by absence or privation of being (Plotinus), the First Intellect (Ibn Sina), a "God of the philosophers" (Whitehead). This abstract God figures in intellectual theologies, humanism and atheism. In the latter, by the "alpha privativum" of the Divine, as in a-theism, an absolute term is produced, but this time by negation instead of by affirmation. God is reduced to an abstract and absolute "no-absolute"—in popular Greek religion, the deities are anthropomorphic.

*Christian model*: God is One essence in Three Persons: God the Father revealed by God's incarnated Son, Jesus Christ, because, in and with God the deifying Holy Spirit. A God of Love, never impersonal, always without evil (pure of heart) and sole cause of goodness (Christianity).

*Oriental model*: God, The All, is One sheer Being present in every part of creation in terms of a manifold of impersonal and personal Divine Self-manifestations (theophanies), as we see in Ancient Egypt, Alexandrian Hermetism (gnosis), Paganism, Hinduism (Vedanta), Jainism, Buddhism, Taoism, Hermeticism.

These approaches underline the multiplicity of the available superstructures or ideologies built on religious life. These meta-languages transform direct experience into indirect or encoded information (traditions), while immediate awareness remains the true touchstone of spirituality. Some of the interpretations and problems will be highlighted which underline the multiplicity ideologies built on religious life.

The outstanding conflict in the theologies of humanity is between those who maintain God's unity is only numerical (i.e. quantitative) and those who understand God to be qualitatively One in All Possible Self-Manifestations of the selfsame God (in Divine Names, Attributes, Gods and Goddesses, the "God of Gods" included). The latter are polytheists only if God's unity is lost, which need not be the case, as history shows and this study tries to point out. Monotheism thinks God solitary. Henotheism thinks God relational. God did literally command the people of God to slaughter men, women and children in the past, but later changed his mind. God changes throughout salvation history; he changed from being a "warrior God" to being a peace-loving God. Problem: Requires discarding doctrine of divine immutability even with regard to God's moral and ethical will.

*Non-literal interpretation:* God did command his people to wage war against certain groups but used hyperbole (or the writers used hyperbole); "men, women, children, cattle, sheep" (etc.) is a figure of speech for completely eliminating the society and culture. Problems: Comes close to allegorical interpretation and there is no record of God's people sparing (e.g., adopting) the children.

*Progressive revelation interpretation:* "Inspiration" does not mean dictation or that every story in the Bible is to be taken at "face value." God accommodated revelation to the people's ability to understand him and people came to understand God's revelation more clearly over time. As God incarnate, Jesus is the clearest revelation of God's character and will. At times God's people misunderstood his command and recorded their own beliefs about God and his commands as revelation from God. God's revelation of his own character and will becomes clearer throughout Scripture with the later (clearer) parts relativizing the earlier (less clear) parts. Problems: Requires a very flexible view of divine inspiration of Scripture (and rejection of inerrancy if not infallibility). Is also subject to accusations of implicit Marcionism.

*Liberal interpretation:* Portions of the Old Testament (and perhaps also of the NT) are culturally conditioned such that they cannot be believed by modern people. The touchstone of biblical interpretation is the modern worldview and modern ethical sensibilities. (In other words, yes, the people of God did slaughter men, women, and children, but God did not command it.). Problem: Sets up a temporal and conditioned cultural norm ("modern") over Scripture itself and possibly even over Jesus himself. Leads to phenomena such as the "Jefferson Bible" (whether literally, physically or not).

A narrative interpretation (not necessarily all narrative approaches agree with this): God included these texts of terror in the canon as a warning to his people about how far it is possible to misunderstand God's will. To what extent they describe actual, historical events is undecideable at this temporal remove and is unimportant. Problem: Implicitly, logically, falls back on either one of the last two above.

*Paradoxical interpretation:* No attempt at harmonization should be exercised; we ought simply to accept at face value the texts of terror and Jesus' teachings about God's love and will (e.g., for peace) and not attempt to diminish either of them or reconcile them. Problem: For inquiring minds leads inevitably to belief in a "hidden

God" (Luther) behind Jesus who willed (and possibly still wills) extreme violence such as genocidal holy war.

The word ecology, economy, and ecumenism originate from the same Greek word oikos. In fact, the human relationship with one another, particularly managing economic resources is an important aspect of ecology (Granberg, 1984). Unfortunately, ecological crisis occurred through the crisis of broken relationship. The misinterpretation of humans created in the image of God gave rise to anthropological supremacy resulting in ecological crisis (White, 1967). He based allegation on the fact that Christianity taught man had dominance over nature so man treated nature in destructive way. He said, "What people do about their ecology depends on what they think about themselves in relation to things around them. Human ecology is deeply conditioned by beliefs about our nature and our destiny—that is, by religion. Worldview will spill over into the external world" (White, 1967:157). Besides, the dualism in philosophy with its outright interplay to theology treating reality as one higher, superior, dominative, and active and the other is considered as lower, inferior, subordinate and passive. Therefore, the environmental crisis is also concerned with the kind of creatures we are and is an outward manifestation of crisis of mind and spirit.

The level of social mobilization and the level of economic development are directly associated with political stability. And this view, of course, varies from one period of time to another period. It also needs to be noted that modernity means stability and modernization instability. For, urbanization, increases in literacy, education, and media exposure all give rise to enhanced aspirations and expectations which, if unsatisfied, galvanize individuals and groups into politics.

This is rightly applicable in the place like in Manipur (North East India). There is ever increase of consciousness in terms of land and its resources. There have been insurgency and militancy movements to claim autonomy and some even *de jure* sovereignty/*de facto* and independence by various ethnic groups (Chiru, 2016). In the absence of strong and adaptable political institutions, such increases in participation mean instability and violence. It is observed that the more modern the society is the more stable and suffers less domestic violence. India has mammoth electorate and successful democracy. However, the rate of development and for whom tends to remain a big question. India has a growth rate of Gross Domestic Product that chases for 9 per cent. But it is doubtful even when this target is achieved India will still have disparities and desperados. With the signing of Pan Naga framework between the Government of India (GoI) and the Nationalist Socialist Council of Nagalim (Isaac-Muiva), the charter of demands ranging from 50 to 100 points wherein included demand for reserved forest which is under the Government of India (GoI). Nagalim (Nagaland, consisting of contiguous Naga inhabited areas) has rich mineral resources (Souvenir, NSCN, 2009). Here in dramatic form can be clearly seen the paradox that modernity produces stability and modernization instability. So the apparent relationship between poverty and backwardness, on the other hand, and stability and violence, on the other, is a spurious one. It is not the absence of modernity but the efforts to achieve it which produce political disorder. Ethnic tribes in the North East India are in the process of modernization. Thus, the definition of modernity and modernization defined. It is not backwardness but modernization that exists to suggest the causes of violence. Now this can be understood likewise: wealthier nations tend to be more stable than those less wealthy, but the poorest nations, those at the bottom of the international economic ladder, tend to be less prone to violence and instability than those countries just above them. Where does my country lie in these three? Whichever may be the case India has strong democratic institutions which act as different from other countries, say that of China? Human rights violation is rampant both in these countries of passing reference compared countries. From the ecological viewpoint justice is a form of authentic and life-enhancing interdependence between man and between society and its environment. With development comes technology. Technology plays an important role in today's world of the 21st century. It either destroys or creates depending on its right application and wrong application. Ian G. Barbour criticizes technology on three different issues: 1. Exploitation of the environment, the exploitative attitudes which have led to environmental deterioration; 2. Reliance on power-military force/equipment which is mainly for destruction; and 3. The impoverishment of experience (Barbour, 2000:85). Rev. J. Thungjamo Lotha in his article cited example of exploitative technology in Nagaland in which before the coming of technology destruction of forests in Nagaland was negligible. But now with the introduction of technologies such as saw mills, veneer mills, plywood factories and the paper and pulp industry, forest in Nagaland are fast disappearing, and the profit of which goes to only a few elite. There are numerous causes of the ecological crisis. This part of the study is concerned about Christian theological perspective and its scientific relational to this as held responsible as anthropocentric. Modern science and technology are products of Western culture, and because Western culture has at its roots from Christian attitudes and principles, and because Christianity is arrogant toward nature and views nature as having no reason for existence except to serve mankind, then Christianity bears burden of guilt for our current ecological crisis. It is referred here to Genesis 1:26-28. From anthropocentric perspective to rule over, to have dominion, or to subdue it, resulted in indiscriminate destruction of nature.

This stewardship of His creation work can best be understood that "Christian stewardship is based on the concept that everything we have was given to us—our health, our emotions, our intellect, our talents, the social and economic benefits into which we have been born, and all we do or earn or make with what God has given us—all ultimately are gifts from God for which we cannot take credit. In fact, God created everything. He owns everything and they are only loan to us. We are not owners but caretakers. And as the Biblical parable of the Talents (Math. 5:14-30) tells us, we will be held accountable to God for what we do with the resources He entrusted to us" (Smith, 2002:52). Care for the environment is Christian concern. The Church and its civil society have sung: "This is my father's world" in which included are all His creation which we have been insulting through misuse of air, water, soil and space. Therefore, Christians are global community that should act as a model in the care for the creation-kingdom ethics for unbelievers and steward the earth as part of worship of God (White, 2006). When the earth is the Lord's and all that is in it, the world, and those who live in it, for He has founded it on the seas, and establish it on the rivers" (Ps. 24:1-2; Deut. 10:14; Lev 25, 23; Gen. 3:20; Ps. 115: 15-16; John 1:3; Acts 14:15; 17:24-26; I Corn. 8:6; Eph. 3:9; I Tim. 6:13, 17).

Ecumenically theology/missiology, especially with regard to an understanding of mission which truly lives up to the Christian conviction that revelation and salvation in Jesus Christ reach the whole creation (colonizer and/or colonized included), every human being and all of humanity, and are thus of universal significance. The marginalized, the excluded, the discriminated are God's people. The Bible rightly pointed that wealth without God has no place in paradise. The example of the rich man and Lazarus is classic one in hermeneutics.

It may be pointed "the way toward finally getting beyond vengeful sorrows and lamentations over our colonial histories, necessary and therapeutic as they have been in our coming to terms with our colonial past and present post-colonial identities, and toward entering a new forum of equality in which we participate as confident dialogic partners in gender (the marginalized and the excluded) terms" (Wan, 2000:111).

In-depth analysis found in the writing of Robert L. Montgomery where it is presented as though missiology is basically a theological discipline, it employs a variety of academic disciplines that use secular methodologies. The social sciences, now increasingly used in missiological research, employ the specifically secular methodologies of science. Historical and Area Studies, traditionally important in missiology, likewise are often if not primarily secular in approach. The two resources, namely secular and theological studies, lead to a three-step approach in producing missiological theory: (1) Identification of questions in missiology in need of missiological theory; (2) Analysis of data obtained through secular disciplines; and (3) Development of missiological theory in which empirical data and theology are woven together. The three-step approach makes it more possible for missiologists to communicate with people in non-theological fields during the second step in order to verify findings.

It also aids people of differing theological perspectives to communicate with each other about empirical realities that are important for missiological theory, as important for producing theory, the nature of the two resources for missiological theory, and the advantages of using a three-step approach in producing missiological theory.

In missiological and hermeneutic linkage to the view of the Northeast Christian tribal, the general approach for the natives with pertinent questions such as how do we understand and re-interpret mission in the light of postcolonial theory and hermeneutics? What crucial missiological challenges can be identified? By connecting the structures of domination and subordination which we are still facing in our churches and the way we are understanding and using difference, post-colonial scholars show that today difference itself has become a category of exclusion and a structural weapon of oppression. How can mission scholars through their theological work contribute to a positive valuation of difference in church and society? In the light of the particular experience of Christians living in religiously divers or "post-Christian" contexts, how do we understand and interpret the encounter between Christians and individuals of other faiths in terms of a postcolonial understanding of mission?

These questions are answered in one word, that Christians are in exilic/exodus imagined society, who supposedly to confront any trouble and sorrows. The difference is not the point of oppression and dominion or domination but rather, it is united colours (call it all dimensions included) of Benetton! The conflict theory has justified such conflict of interest between individuals and groups. Christians are to bring justice through righteousness. God works through the oppressions from the dominant groups. For instance, in world Biblical history, as in the case of Israelites, from the slavery of Egyptians. The small England as is rightly described by Pandit Nehru that it is not the size but something else that made England the conqueror of the world as a Christian nation. Though whether explorers or merchants or chaplains were no righteous but few in private capacities the political agents of the British rendered a yeoman service to Christianity in India as anywhere else. It was William Wilberforce and the like-minded people who could bring such an Act as that of Charter Act of 1813 for missionisation in India. The civil society and the church differences are part and parcel of conflict theory as academically understood of Marx who has no God, but in reality before Marx various literature of religions and civilizations had already seen the similar nature of conflicts that amounted to full-fledged wars and destruction which consequently contributed whether one likes it or not a new paradigm or a new society which may contain both pros and cons. Christians are not to yoke with other faiths but no harm in joke. Christians are not to show long faces to other faiths but if at all it must be from the uselessness of the vanities of the world or ills of the fore-fathers traditional practices including no fables and old wife tales and gossips. This does not meant in the context of the targeted populace of the study that they completely do away with the folk tales and folk lore which form the social anthropological and sociological approaches to their traditions and culture that is counted as their identity and nationalism. But as Christians are supposed to be serious about their faith that liberated them from sin and death. So sin and death is no laughing matter! The x-ray/ultrasound machines do not recognize the exterior beauty and additional cosmetic or otherwise in a person who undergo the process of filming the ailment in the body when getting sick. That is why repeatedly the Bible warns of external shows and beatification. Here the analogy of the physician looking for cure of a patient is a fit case to cite. To administer cure he has to identify causes of the ailment. The same holds true in cure of the approaches to address the confrontation of the causes of colonization and liberation.

Liberation, in the political context and the missiological and hermeneutics concept. The Christians are to manifest the true nature of whom they follow. Of which is care for the poor and needy in the true spirit of care for others more than what he expects from others or in other words, do unto others as you wish to be done by! North East Christian tribal were colonized but with it came many benefits in the form of Christian education which was received reluctantly and with stiff resistance. Whatever was the characterized mode of reception, they somehow received education and medical needs from the Western missionaries, of which many scholars argue that the missionaries converted the natives with the ulterior motive of civilizing the uncivilized imposing Western culture at the cost of making the natives disowned their culture and tradition. However the study attempts this issue with the contextualization approach adopted in Christian mission and approach.

How do we read the Bible and other religious texts by means of a post-colonial hermeneutics? Applied to the theory and practice of scriptural reading, a post-colonial perspective exposes how Biblical studies and the Biblical texts themselves have been used in support of imperialist and patriarchal agendas. From a missiological point of view, this is an invitation to re-visit especially those Biblical texts that have informed the theories and practices of Christian mission and to search for alternative readings which overcome any exclusivist stance (this is where inclusivist approach is applicable) and offer liberating perspectives of dialogue and solidarity across different cultures, social locations and faith traditions. Christians are to apply the theories which form time to time the world and the systems are changing but still the Bible is relevant for all times under any form of man-made governments. Slavery was practiced in the old testament of the Bible however in the New Testament of the Bible it was made slave to sin and to be a free man. A new creation in Jesus Christ means not looking back the past misdeeds and sins. Detesting what is evil not the sinner. Slavery and bonded labour is prohibited in the post-colonial world but in similar form of exploitation committed by the dominant over the weak. Patriarchy is practiced everywhere in the world. But does this practice restrict the fairer sex from emancipation and empowerment? No. In fact women are projected as one same flesh and blood in matrimony. They are termed partners or co-workers. In fact, Apostle John in Revelation wrote that on the Judgment Day in the New Heavens there will be no male or female before the throne of grace. Apostle Paul discreetly and exhaustively wrote of his opinion on the relationship between all members of the family. This is applicable to the extended universal family. As he said that one should treat older woman as his own mother or sister as the case applies. So is the case with the male.

Regarding the history of mission, post-colonial theory provides a reading technique that may reveal the agency of marginalised, both from the "sending" churches and from the "receiving" missions, at different levels in this history. How must missionary archives be read in order to give importance to the marginalized, whose work has been forgotten, especially of the indigenous communities? How has the history of mission to be re-written in order to recreate the stories of the indigenous communities and their ways to live as people of faith? Are there stories of early community building, of the creative agency, stories of resistance and hope who have to be told in order to better understand the challenges faced as of faith in multicultural and multi-religious contexts today?

By emphasising the need of critical exchange and mutual transformation instead of clinging to stereotyped attributions, the perspective of post-colonial subjects invites us to situate ourselves in this global world, to acknowledge the differences between us and to begin seeking common ground across these differences. How do we deal with the differences and divides between dominant theologians (including non-academic dominated of faith) in various parts of the world, in the light of post-colonial theory and hermeneutics? How do we maintain the integrity, the particularity, and the diversity of the various traditions and mission understandings? How do we find the spaces of justice and liberating interdependence (Dube, 2000) where new coalitions can be built? (The functional approaches is applicable here). How do we collaborate in theological research and teaching projects in such a post-colonial context?

The intention here is to include systematic, Biblical and historical perspectives, compare and contrast cultures around the world, discussing topics such as: the nature of culture, race and ethnicity, making a living in the environment, gender and marriage, family and kinship, stratification and poverty, political and economic systems, language, culture and personality, religion, the arts and world-views. A Christian framework will provide the means of determining both the value and limits of cultural relativism.

Church does mission and mission is for the sake of planting and building the church—carry-over of Rufus Anderson's theory of a three-self movement of self-governing, self-propagating, self-sustaining churches. A focusing Biblical text: Matt 28: 19-20: "Go therefore and make disciples of all nations, baptizing them in the name of the Father and of the Son and of the Holy Spirit, and teaching them to obey everything that I have commanded you. And remember, I am with you always, to the end of the age."

God is a missionary God, people therefore are missionary; church is sent by God. A focusing Biblical text: John 17: 20-21: "I ask not only on behalf of these, but also on behalf of those who will believe in me through their word, that they may all be one. As you, Father, are in me and I am in you, may they also be in us, so that the world may believe that you have sent me." Emphasis on God as a missionary God-mission from the nature of God, attribute of God-trinity is a model of mission.

Emphasis on unity of the church—because it is God's mission we all participate with God. A focusing Biblical text: Luke 4: 16-21: "When he came to Nazareth, where he had been brought up, he went to the synagogue on the Sabbath day, as was his custom. He stood up to read, and the scroll of the prophet Isaiah was given to him. He unrolled the scroll and found the place where it was written: The Spirit of the Lord is upon me, because he has anointed me to bring good news to the poor. He has sent me to proclaim release to the captives and recovery of sight to the blind, to let the oppressed go free, to proclaim the year of the Lord's favour" (Luke 4:18-19). And he rolled up the scroll, gave it back to the attendant and sat down. The eyes of all in the synagogue were fixed on him. Then he began to say to them, 'Today this scripture has been fulfilled in your hearing' (Luke 4:21). Post-colonial and missiological approaches in the context of the tribals of the North East Indian Christians can be automatically linked to the preservation of the ethnic culture and languages as their identity and nationalism at the same time addressing them in the post-modern world, cosmopolitism, and other applicable theories relevant for them. In missiology and hermeneutics Christ did say that he came not to destroy the Moses Law but to fulfil it. These theories are grounded on the social realities of the society. Missiological theory emphasise that the contextual study is essential to address the given societal context. Therefore, due importance to study of tradition and culture of the Christian tribals of the North East India is of outmost priority in this study. The constitution of India recognizes that and incorporated the freedom to protect and promote such traditions and culture. The tradition and culture of this region must be incorporated in the missiolocal and hermeneutics of the Christians of the tribal communities of North East India. If arts and culture in the form of paintings of the this region does not reveal such, though many non-Christians arts may also have connections as much as secular theories of sociology and other social sciences and sciences included are deploy in any theorization. The point of discussion here is not so much on how these theories are from which sources but are they relevant in its application in the region. If not applicable, can we think of new paradigm? Yes, why not. The tribal Christians from the North East India possess all the elements or components to theorize theology of their own in the contextualization. If say for instance, muster seed of Middle East is different from the North East Indian context there is no harm to contextualize with our own vegetation. So is the case of sheep, which is seldom seen here in such large scale form that of the Middle East. Neither do we have olive tree but we can contextualize with similar medicinal plants available in the North East region? The purpose of the theorized forms of missiological and hermeneutics from the North East India perspective is to apply that is relevant for this region. Duly given the tradition and culture of this region, Christ came to reconcile all these differences as a mediator. The social contextualization and the preservation of the cultural and social practices in the North East India by the Colonial and Independent India can be located in the way even now the region is still different from the mainland India in all spheres.

The theories discussed here are very much applicable in some way or the other to the North East Indian Christian tribal as is defined in the constitution of India. Prior to the advent of Christianity in the North East India, the tribal were administered by the British India with the mechanism fit to them as they were far off, though physically a stone throw away distance with the plainsmen, especially in terms of their culture, language, and religion. The Tribal traditional faith and worship was negative in nature. Their faith and worship was based on their imagination that there was omnipotent, omnipresent, and omniscient. They never worship idols. The question of the applicability of a fulfilment approach to other religions either by the colonial Indian towards the colonized (debated that only through missionisation the tribes were tamed not otherwise) or now the independent North East India tribal Christians in its relation to other faiths can be summed up in D' Costa words that gives a fine review of the perspectives at work in the church from the time of the early fathers through to the Second Vatican Council observing that until the twentieth century there has generally been what might be called a salvation pessimism about the salvation of non-Christians, that is, there is an assumption that because of sin non-Christians will be lost. Our recent history can be characterized by a move to a salvation optimism, which is always in danger of playing down the power of sin and exalting the power of human goodness. A new hermeneutical context which contextualizes this tradition; that well until the age of discovery in the fifteenth century it was generally assumed by most theologians that after the time of Christ everyone knew the gospel. If a person was not a Christian they had explicitly rejected the truth of God. This meant that Judaism and eventually Islam (from the seventh century on) were both seen as heretical and/or schismatic movements, rather than genuinely "other" as we tend to view these and other traditions today.

## Emphasis on Reconciliation

### *Church for Others Section*

Identification of Christ with human situation—identification of Christians with people they wished to serve and witness to—personal encounter, open expectant attitude toward others; there is an interdependence between people and nations in the world community. We need to dialogue to work together to meet human necessities, relieve human suffering, establish social justice, share in the struggle for peace.

Development process (education, human rights, sexism, racism)—secular bodies have the main responsibility for this.

Christians are "to assist in the definition, validation, and articulation of just political, economic and social objectives and in translating them into action" (Brajamani, 2003, 119). The criterion for these objectives was a sustainable global society, solidarity with poor and oppressed as central priority in Christian mission—identification of Jesus with the poor, divine judgment on oppressors.

There are aspects within each culture that deny life and oppress people—celebrate a plurality of cultures. Because they share common human aspirations and responsibility for others, Christians ought to engage in dialogue with those also concerned about ultimate questions of renew the whole creation. Concluding analysis here included: through our acceptance of the ministry of reconciliation, we become a missionary people, not in that sense of dominating over peoples and nations which has all too often characterized mission work, but in the sense of sharing God's own mission of brining all humanity into communion with God through Christ in the power of the Spirit, sharing our faith and our resources with all people.

### *Mission and Inculturation*

The church is called to be a light to all nations, but also to respect the dignity of every human person, including their freedom of conscience. It must plant Christian communities in every nation, incorporating into the Church anything that is good, true, and holy in the cultures of the world, which requires keen discernment. Inculturation must not become uncritical assimilation. In that process, as John Paul II stated in his *Encyclical Faith and Reason*, "the Church cannot abandon what she has gained from her inculturation in the world of Greco-Latin thought. To reject this heritage would be to deny the providential plan of God who guides his Church down the paths of time and history" (Fides et Ratio, 1998:72).

### *Social Justice*

From a universal Christian perspective, the relationship between religions is profoundly oriented towards the common good, and this is one of the major reasons for interreligious dialogue. In seeking to advance human well-being in contexts where other religions are dominant, D' Costa thinks that we should argue from within the other's tradition whenever possible. But when this fails, dialectical argument against the religion is required. The next step may be to resort to international political pressure, but Christians must bear suffering rather than resort to violence.

As mentioned about the tribal areas (Excluded or partially excluded the terms used till 1935 leading to Independent India famous Sixth Schedule of the constitution of India) the tribals of the North East India has a special provision which has tax exemption in rural areas except that they are supposed to contribute through the state government concern to uplift the downtrodden with the central fund earmarked for the amelioration and elimination of poverty and diseases. Educational standard is picking up though exponentially lacking behind the national average. The Government of India has incorporated in the country's document that welfare of the Scheduled Castes and Tribes in all aspects. There is special provision for the tribals from the North East that in certain areas such as culture and religious practices domain, the State Assemblies have been delegated power to decide what is deemed fit to be applied in the interest of the tribals. In certain states like Manipur, Hill Area Committee had been created to look after the affairs of the tribals in the Hills. Economically, the tribals from the North East India contributed in the exchange mechanism of trade and commerce. Tribal belts products are in the plains markets in the states of the North East India. They contribute a large chunk of labour force too. In the light of integrity of the administrative areas, the fabric of cohesion and co-existence has been questioned by the tribes because of poor budget allocation to the tribals, particularly in Manipur. The demand for separate administrative mechanism has been the disturbing issue as piece-meal grant by the government in power that from time to time derailed the peaceful co-existence. For which conflict theory will suffice. But as to functional approach, since the static approach is being advocated, whatever has been enshrined in the constitution of the land has been more or less of welfare services and public sector in nature. Though in the past more than a decade privatization and liberalization has played quite a different role as part of the public-private synergy in all sectors of the economy in the North East India. In this regard, the contribution of the youths in multinational and private companies in major cities in India is phenomenally high.

The functionalist perspective is more or less of welfarist approach where citizen is groomed as obedient or loyal in performing duties as demanded from, from generation to another. It held the view that each aspect of society is interdependent and contributes to society's functioning as a whole. The government, or state, provides education for the children of the family, which in turn pays taxes on which the state depends to keep itself running. That is, the family is dependent upon the school to help children grow up to have good jobs so that they can raise and support their own families. In the process, the children become law-abiding, taxpaying citizens, who in turn support the state. If all goes well, the parts of society produce order, stability, and productivity. If all does not go well, the parts of society then must adapt to recapture a new order, stability, and productivity. For example, during a financial recession with its high rates of unemployment and inflation, social programmes are trimmed or cut. Schools offer fewer programmes. Families tighten their budgets. And a new social order, stability, and productivity occur has received criticism for neglecting the negative functions of an event such as divorce. Critics also claim that the perspective justifies the status quo and complacency on the part of society's members. Functionalism does not encourage people to take an active role in changing their social environment, even when such change may benefit them. Instead, functionalism sees active social change as undesirable because the various parts of society will compensate naturally for any problems that may arise.

## Summarizing the Theorized Paradigm for Christian Tribals of the North East India

1. Therefore looking at the prism of the social aspects sociological theories as discussed in this concluding chapter can rightly reveal that all what has been discussed either through the interactive, functional, and of conflict theory, are applicable in the tribal way of

society in the globalized world. In terms of the nature of economy, the tribal society are of the nature of both socialistic and capitalistic. Individual and community/clan or both are practiced in the North East tribal society. Therefore, whichever is the case applicable, sociological theories are helpful in containing the tribal demand for conflict resolution through the proper management and redressal in the aspirations of the tribal people in the region? From time to time, the authority in power would love to talk about law and order problem of the North Eastern states. However, in the context of tribal aspirations for administrative mechanism, it is the political will to decide what type of fit case demand can be granted depending on the wisdom and statesmanship of the Indian leaders in dialogue with the partners for associated mutual benefits.

2. It is very interesting to notice that the region continues to maintain its own cultural and linguistic identity despite imposition of Western culture by the missionaries in some way or the other, reluctant to call it so though. Many British anthropologists and social anthropologists like Verrier Elwin, H.H. Hutton, Henry Balfour, J.P. Mills and so on, are of the view that Christianity transformed at the cost of destroying the tribal culture. North East Indian tribal society to the extent that they vehemently critique the Western culture of industrialized economy and way of living.

3. In-depth analysis found in the writing of Robert L. Montgomery where it is presented as though missiology is basically a theological discipline; it employs a variety of academic disciplines that use secular methodologies. The social sciences, now increasingly used in missiological research, employ the specifically secular methodologies of science. Historical and Area Studies, traditionally important in missiology, likewise are often if not primarily secular in approach. The two resources, namely secular and theological studies, lead to a three-step approach in producing missiological theory: (1) Identification of questions in missiology in need of missiological theory; (2) Analysis of data obtained through secular disciplines; and (3) Development of missiological theory in which empirical data and theology are woven together. The three-step approach makes it more possible for missiologists to communicate with people in non-

theological fields during the second step in order to verify findings. It also aids people of differing theological perspectives to communicate with each other about empirical realities that are important for missiological theory, as important for producing theory, the nature of the two resources for missiological theory, and the advantages of using a three-step approach in producing missiological theory.

4. In missiological and hermeneutic linkage to the view of the North East Christian tribal, the general approach for the natives with pertinent questions such as how do we understand and re-interpret mission in the light of post-colonial theory and hermeneutics? What crucial missiological challenges can be identified? By connecting the structures of domination and subordination which we are still facing in our churches and the way we are understanding and using difference, post-colonial scholars show that today difference itself has become a category of exclusion and a structural weapon of oppression. How can mission scholars through their theological work contribute to a positive valuation of difference in church and society? In the light of the particular experience of Christians living in religiously diverse or "post-Christian" contexts, how do we understand and interpret the encounter between Christians and individuals of other faiths in terms of a post-colonial understanding of mission? These questions are answered in one word, that Christians are in exilic/exodus imagined society, who supposedly to confront any trouble and sorrows. The difference is not the point of oppression and dominion or domination but rather, it is united colours (call it all dimensions included) of Benetton! The conflict theory has justified such conflict of interest between individuals and groups. Christians are to bring justice through righteousness. God works through the oppressions from the dominant groups. For instance, in world Biblical history, as in the case of Israelites, from the slavery of Egyptians.

5. How do we read the Bible and other religious texts by means of a post-colonial hermeneutics? Applied to the theory and practice of scriptural reading, a post-colonial perspective exposes how Biblical studies and the Biblical texts themselves have been used in support of imperialist and patriarchal agendas. From a missiological point of view, this is an invitation to re-visit especially those Biblical texts

that have informed the theories and practices of Christian mission and to search for alternative readings which overcome any exclusivist stance (this is where inclusivist approach is applicable) and offer liberating perspectives of dialogue and solidarity across different cultures, social locations and faith traditions. Christians are to apply the theories which from time to time the world and the systems are changing but still the Bible is relevant for all times under any form of man-made governments.

## References

Ahmed, Mehtabuddin and Chowdury, Prosenjit (eds.) (1996). *The Turbulent North East*, New Delhi.

Bhattacharyya, N.N. (1995). *Religious Culture of North-Eastern India*, New Delhi: Manohar Publishers & Distributors.

Bhaumik, Subir (1996). *Insurgent Cross Fire: North-East India*, New Delhi: Lancer Publishers.

Bhuyan, Arun Chandan and De Sibopada, (eds.) (1999). *Political History of Assam*, Vol. II 1920-1939, Guwahati: Publication Board Assam.

Bosh, David J. (2005). *Transforming Mission: Paradigm Shifts in Theology of Mission*, New York: Orbit book.

Brajamani, S. (2003). *Economic Growth in Manipur: An Empirical Analysis*, Manipur: S. Romesh Singh.

Brown, R. (2001). *Statistical Account of Manipur*, New Delhi: Mittal Publications.

Chasie, Charles (1999). *The Naga Imbroglio: A Personal Perspective*, Kohima: Standard Printers & Publishers.

Chiru, S.S. (2007). *American Baptist Mission: An Integrating Agent of the Nagas into Indian Union*, New Delhi: Sunrise Publications.

Das, Samir Kumar (1997). *Regionalism in Power*, New Delhi: Omsons Publications.

Dube, Musa W. *Postcoloniality, Feminist Spaces and Religion,* In: Laura E. Donaldson/Kwok.

Ghose, Sumita (ed.) (1998). *Sanjoy's Assam: Diaries and Writings of Sanjoy Ghose*, New Delhi: Penguin Books.

Gohain, U.N. (1942). *Assam Under the Ahoms*, Guwahati: Spectrum Publications.

Hazarika, Sanjoy (2000). *Rites Passage: Border Crossings*, Imagined Homelands, India's East and Bangladesh, New Delhi: Penguin Books.

Hudson, T.C. (1911). *The Naga Tribes of Manipur*, New Delhi: Low Price Publications.

Hume, David (1998). *Dialogues Concerning Natural Religion*, 2nd edition, Indianapolis: Hackett.

Hunter, W.W. (1879). *A Statistical Account of Assam,* Vol. I, Guwahati: Delhi: Spectrum Publications.

Hutton, J.H. (2003). *The Angami Nagas*, Nagaland: Directorate of Art and Culture.

Iralu, Kaka, D. (2000). *Nagaland and India: The Blood and the Tears*, Kohima: Published by Kaka, D. Iralu.

Johnstone, James (2002). *Manipur and the Naga Hills*, New Delhi: Gyan Publishing House.

Kamson, M. (2004). *A North East Report*, Second Scheduled Areas and Scheduled Tribes Commission Report, New Delhi.

Kumar, B.B. (1995). *Tensions and Conflict in North East India*, New Delhi: Cosmo Publications.

Kumar, Nikhilesh (1999). *Survey of Research in Sociology and Social Anthropology in North-East India (1970-1990)*, New Delhi: Regency Publications.

Lal, Dena (ed.) (1991). *History of Modern Manipu— 1826-1949*, New Delhi: Orbit Publishers-Distributors.

Litty Russell (1974). *Human Liberation in a Feminist Perspective: A Theology*. Philadelphia: The Westminster Press.

Luthra, P.N. (1974). *Nagaland: From a District to a State*, Shillong: Director of Information and Public Relations.

Maitra, Kiranshankar (2002). *The Noxious Web: Insurgency in the North East*, New Delhi: Kanishka Publishers, Distributors.

Mills, J.P. (1982). *The Rengma Nagas*, Nagaland: Directorate of Art and Culture, Government of Nagaland.

Mills, J.P. (2003). *The Ao Nagas*, Nagaland: Directorate of Art and Culture, Government of Nagaland.

Mooney, Knox, and Schacht (2006). *Understanding Social Problems*, 5th edition "National Consultation on Draft National Tribal Policy", New Delhi.

Namo, Dalle (1987). *The Prisoner From Nagaland*, Nagaland: United Publisher.

Nuh, V.K. (2001). *Struggle for Identity in North-East India: A Theological Response*, Guwahati: New Delhi: Spectrum Publications.

Nuh, V.K. (2002). *My Native Country: The Land of the Nagas*, Guwahati: Delhi: Spectrum Publications.

Pakem, B. (1997). *Insurgency in North East India*, New Delhi: Om Sons Publications.

Pui-lan (ed.) (2002). *Postcolonialism, Feminism and Religious Discourse*, New York.

Sachdeva, Rajesh (ed.) (2001). *Language Education in Nagaland: Sociolinguistic Dimensions*, New Delhi: Regency Publications.

Singh, Bhupinder (2002). *Autonomy Movements and Federal India,* Jaipur & New Delhi: Rawat Publications.

Smith, W.C. (2002). *The Ao Naga Tribe of Assam*, New Delhi: Mittal Publications.

Srivastav, Nirankar (2000). *Survey of Research in Economics on North East India — 1970-1990*, New Delhi: Regency Publications.

Thomas, C. Joshua and Das Gurudas, (2002). *Dimensions of Development in Nagaland*, New Delhi: Regency Publications.

Zehol, Lucy (1998). *Ethnicity in Manipur: Experience, Issues and Perspectives*, New Delhi: Regency Publications.

Zehol, Lucy (2001). *Research Priorities in North East India: With Special Reference to Manipur*, New Delhi: Regency Publications.

# Index